FOREWORD

IN 1939 the prospect of a war which would involve many Asian nations made men in positions of responsibility in Britain suddenly aware of the meagre number of our experts in Asian languages and cultures. The Scarbrough Commission was set up, and its report led to a great expansion of Oriental and African studies in Britain after the war. In the third decade after 1939 events are making clear to ever-widening circles of readers the need for something more than a superficial knowledge of non-European cultures. In particular the blossoming into independence of numerous African states, many of which are largely Muslim or have a Muslim head of state, emphasises the growing political importance of the Islamic world, and, as a result, the desirability of extending and deepening the understanding and appreciation of this great segment of mankind. Since history counts for much among Muslims, and what happened in 632 or 656 may still be a live issue, a journalistic familiarity with present conditions is not enough; there must also be some awareness of how the past has moulded the present.

This series of 'Islamic surveys' is designed to give the educated reader something more than can be found in the usual popular books. Each work undertakes to survey a special part of the field, and to show the present stage of scholarship here. Where there is a clear picture this will be given, but where there are gaps, obscurities and differences of opinion, these will also be indicated. Comprehensive bibliographies will afford guidance to those who want to pursue their studies further. In the present volume there is bibliographical material on pp. xi, 81f., 105-7, and also in the notes, pp. 135-44.

The transliteration of Arabic words is essentially that of the second edition of *The Encyclopaedia of Islam* (London, 1960, continuing) with three modifications. Two of these are normal with most British Arabists, namely, *q* for *ḳ*, and *j* for *dj*. The third is something of a novelty. It is the replacement of the ligature used to show when two consonants are to be sounded together by an apostrophe to show when they are to be sounded separately. This means that *dh*, *gh*, *kh*, *sh*, *th* (and in non-Arabic words *ch* and *zh*) are to be sounded together; where there is an apostrophe, as in *ad'ham*, they are to be sounded separately. The apostrophe in this usage represents no sound, but, since it only occurs between two consonants (of which the second is *h*), it cannot be confused with the apostrophe representing the glottal stop (*hamza*), which never occurs between two consonants.

W. Montgomery Watt
GENERAL EDITOR

WASSERSTROM

ISLAMIC SURVEYS 6

ISLAMIC POLITICAL THOUGHT

The Basic Concepts

W. MONTGOMERY WATT

EDINBURGH
at the University Press

EDINBURGH UNIVERSITY PRESS
22 George Square, Edinburgh

First Published 1968
Paperback edition 1980
ISBN 0 85224 403 7

Printed in Great Britain by
Clark Constable Ltd
Edinburgh

CONTENTS

Introduction ix

CHAPTER ONE. The Islamic State under Muḥammad
1. Muḥammad's political achievements 3
2. The Constitution of Medina 4
3. The pre-Islamic tribe and the Medinan state 6
4. The nature of the community 9
5. The Jihād or 'holy war' 14

CHAPTER TWO. Muḥammad as Head of State
1. Muḥammad's position under the Constitution 20
2. Muḥammad's position in the later Medinan period 23
3. The political relevance of religion 26

CHAPTER THREE. The Early Caliphate
1. The situation at Muḥammad's death 31
2. The succession to the caliphate 35
3. The nature of the caliphate 40
4. The first appearance of Shīʿite ideas 42

CHAPTER FOUR. The Organization of Empire
1. The Muslims as a military élite 46
2. The 'protected minorities' 49
3. Provincial administration 52

CHAPTER FIVE. Membership of the Community
1. The Khārijite movement 54
2. The wider community of true believers 57
3. The conditions of membership of the community 59

CHAPTER SIX. The Religious Institution
1. The formation of the religious institution 64
2. The formation of the Islamic world-view 67
3. The religious institution and the rulers 73

CHAPTER SEVEN. The Form of the Political Struggle
1. The Persian imperial tradition 78
2. The power struggle under the first ʿAbbāsids 82
3. The intellectual form of the struggle 85

CHAPTER EIGHT. The Community as Bearer of Values
1. The nature and purpose of the community 90
2. Ideals and laws 93
3. The community and the individual 96

CHAPTER NINE. War-lords and Political Theorists
1. The emergence of the war-lords 99
2. The political theorists 101
Appended note: A preliminary list of political theorists 104
3. The caliphate after 1258 107

CHAPTER TEN. The Development of Shīʿite Islam
1. 'Moderate' Shīʿism and the Imāmite party 110
2. Revolutionary or 'Sevener' Shīʿism 112
3. Zaydite Shīʿism 114

CHAPTER ELEVEN. Epilogue: Islam in Contemporary Politics
1. Islam and occidental political ideas 116
(*a*) Nationalism 116
(*b*) Democracy, totalitarianism, and socialism 120
2. Actualizing possibilities of adaptation 123

APPENDIX. The Constitution of Medina 130

NOTES 135

INDEX, by Peter McIntyre 145

INTRODUCTION

By the year AD 2000 it seems probable that Islam will be one of the half-dozen significant political forces in the world. The others will be Lenino-marxism, Confucio-marxism, probably Catholic Christianity, probably an amalgam of humanism and Protestant Christianity, and Buddhism, perhaps in some sort of alliance with Hinduism. To many Europeans and Americans it may seem strange to include religions among political forces, because they have been accustomed to think of religion as concerned only with personal piety. They are misled, however, by the divorce of religion and politics in the West since the European wars of religion in the sixteenth and seventeenth centuries. Throughout the vast ranges of world history it has been normal for religion to be closely linked with politics. The reason is not far to seek. When politics becomes serious and it is a question of men being ready to die for the cause they support, there has to be some deep driving force in their lives. Usually this force can be supplied only by a religion, or by an ideology that is acquiring some of the functions of religion (such as making man aware of the powers on which his life is dependent). This question of the relation of religion and politics will concern us further in the course of the study.

My aim in what follows is to show the roots or genesis of the political conceptions operative in the Islamic world today. In this region of the world it is particularly necessary to look at the past, since for Muslims as for Irishmen history is still alive. The Islamic community is still divided by events that took place in 632 and 656. A remark about an incident concerning one of Muḥammad's wives in the year 627, when made in the Sudan in 1965, led to riots and the declaration that the Communist party was illegal. Thus a study of the distant past is not purely academic. This is especially so since we shall be studying practice more than theory. In the Islamic world the concepts implicit in men's practice are more important than the writings of political theorists. There are indeed some of the latter, and they will be looked at in due course; but it will be found that they are of secondary importance.

This study is thus primarily concerned with Islamic political ideas as they have been operative in the historical process. It cannot avoid reference to the religious ideas with which the political ideas are closely linked, but it will attempt to preserve the neutrality proper to the social scientist; that is to say, it will neither affirm nor deny the metaphysical truth of the religious ideas, but will consider them as ideas influencing the life of society.

Bibliographical note

No single work altogether covers the ground of the present study. The following deal with important sections of the subject-matter.

CAHEN, Claude: 'The Body Politic', in G. E. von Grunebaum (ed.), *Unity and Variety in Muslim Civilization*, Chicago, 1955, 132-58. A valuable review of the subject.

GARDET, Louis: *La cité musulmane, vie sociale et politique*, Paris, 1954. The fullest recent systematic presentation, though based more on the political theorists than on actual practice; deals also with contemporary problems.

GAUDEFROY-DEMOMBYNES, Maurice: *Muslim Institutions*, London, 1950, esp. chs. 1, 'The Muslim Dominion'; 2, 'The Muslim Community'; 7, 'The Caliphate'.

LEVY, Reuben: *The Social Structure of Islam*, Cambridge, 1957; esp. ch. 7, 'The Caliphate and the Central Government' (pp. 271-354), and ch. 8, 'Government in the Provinces' (pp. 355-406).

MACDONALD, Duncan Black: *Development of Muslim Theology, Jurisprudence and Constitutional Theory*, New York, 1903; part I (7-63) 'Constitutional Development'; chiefly historical and now partly out of date.

MEZ, Adam: *The Renaissance of Islam* (tr. by S. Khuda Bakhsh and D. S. Margoliouth), Patna, 1937; pp. 1-234 contain relevant material.

VON GRUNEBAUM, Gustav E.: *Medieval Islam*, Chicago, 1946, etc., esp. chs. 4, 5, 'The Body Politic: Law and the State'; 'The Social Order' (pp. 142-220).

VON KREMER, Alfred: *Geschichte der herrschenden Ideen des Islams*, Leipzig, 1868, etc., esp. Book 3, 'Die Staatsidee des Islams' (pp. 309-467); partly historical.

ISLAMIC POLITICAL THOUGHT

ONE

THE ISLAMIC STATE UNDER MUḤAMMAD

1. Muḥammad's political achievements

About the year AD 610 the town of Mecca, near the centre of the west coast of Arabia, had a population of a thousand or so men capable of bearing arms, perhaps rather more than 5000 people in all. Mecca was a prosperous commercial centre. The great merchants there controlled all the trade passing up and down the Arabian west coast route, which at this time was perhaps the chief artery between the Indian Ocean (including its African shores) and the Mediterranean. They also traded with Iraq, then part of the Persian empire, and controlled mining and other enterprises along or near the various routes. When one of the citizens of Mecca in the middle ranks of merchants began to communicate to other citizens messages from what he claimed to be a supernatural source, it seemed unlikely that this would affect the commercial and political life of Mecca. A hard-headed business man was unlikely to be unduly upset by threats of punishment in Hell or of some more tangible temporal disaster. Even if some of the merchants made a slight response to the appeal to be less niggardly with their wealth, this was unlikely to influence the town's trade significantly. In short, the religious movement begun by Muḥammad had no obvious political relevance.

Nevertheless the great merchants of Mecca in time became afraid of Muḥammad and his religious movement. Muḥammad's contemporaries in particular saw that his claim to be the bearer of divine truth was a potential basis for political interference, since the ordinary citizen was likely to think that Muḥammad knew better than those who had no access to such a source of wisdom. Moreover the modern observer is able to see that, though Muḥammad's proclamations were primarily religious, the religious ideas they contained were a response to the total situation in Mecca. Commercial prosperity had led to deep social malaise among the Meccans. Perhaps the chief tension was that between the necessities of commercial life on the one hand and, on the other, the nomadic mores and nomadic ideas still influencing most of the inhabitants. The religious ideas of the Qur'ān were directed towards the religious roots of the contemporary malaise; but the malaise was linked with the whole economic and social life of the Meccans.[1] It is not surprising that Muḥammad met with opposition, even though, so long as he remained at Mecca, the political potential of the Qur'ānic ideas remained unrealized.

Muḥammad's Hijra or migration to Medina in 622 marks the beginning of his political activity. It was not that he suddenly acquired great political power, for in fact his power grew very gradually; but the agreements into which he entered with the clans of Medina meant the establishment of a new body politic, and within this body there was scope for realizing the political potentialities of the Qur'ānic ideas. By 624 Muḥammad and the Muslims of Medina were involved in hostilities with the pagan Meccans. Despite the initial superiority of the latter the final outcome was the virtually unopposed occupation of Mecca by Muḥammad in 630. A week or two later he defeated a concentration of nomadic tribes at Ḥunayn; and this meant that no one in Arabia was now capable of meeting him in battle with any hope of success. From most parts of Arabia tribes or sections of tribes sent representatives to Medina seeking alliance with him. By the time of his death in June 632, despite rumblings of revolt, he was in control of much of Arabia. The Islamic state had no precisely defined geographical frontiers, but it was certainly in existence.

2. The Constitution of Medina

In the main early source (apart from the Qur'ān) for the career of Muḥammad there is found a document which may conveniently be called 'the Constitution of Medina'. The interpretation of this document raises various problems which cannot be discussed here. The general view to be adopted, however, may be summarized under the following points: (*a*) the document is not a unitary one, but is a conflation of at least two distinct documents, as is shown by the repetition or virtual repetition of several articles; (*b*) in its present form the document dates from after 627, by which time the three main Jewish clans (Qaynuqāʿ, an-Naḍīr and Qurayẓa) had been expelled or executed – the two latter clans do not appear to be mentioned in the document, but it is known that there were some small groups of Jews in Medina after 627; (*c*) the chief provisions probably go back to the time of the Hijra in 622 or at least to 624, but articles which had ceased to be relevant may have been omitted or modified, while others may have been added.[2] Such a view justifies the use of the material in the Constitution in a study of the nature of the Medinan state. On the other hand, if scholars manage to prove an earlier date, any conclusions reached on the basis of this view will not be seriously affected.

Some of the articles in the Constitution deal with minor matters, while others are repetitive. The essential points defining the nature of the state (apart from the functions and privileges of the head of state) are the following:

(1) The believers and their dependents constitute a single community (*umma*).
(2) Each clan or subdivision of the community is responsible for blood-money and ransoms on behalf of its members (arts. 2-11).
(3) The members of the community are to show complete solidarity against crime and not to support a criminal even when he is a near kinsman, where the crime is against another member of the community (arts. 13, 21).
(4) The members of the community are to show complete solidarity against the unbelievers in peace and war (arts. 14, 17, 19, 44), and also solidarity in the granting of 'neighbourly protection' (art. 15).
(5) The Jews of various groups belong to the community, and are to retain their own religion; they and the Muslims are to render 'help' (including military aid) to one another when it is needed (arts. 24-35, 37, 38, 46).

Before we discuss these points in more detail the general comment may be made that this document is no invention of a political theorist, but is rooted in the mentality and mores of pre-Islamic Arabia. So any consideration of the nature of the Islamic state must begin by looking at the political conceptions which guided the activities of the pre-Islamic Arabs.

3. The pre-Islamic tribe and the Medinan state

A distinctive feature of pre-Islamic tribal life was the maintenance of security by a high degree of social solidarity. The most familiar aspect of this is the *lex talionis* of 'an eye for an eye, a tooth for a tooth, and a life for a life'.[3] Occidental readers, perhaps influenced by the well-known New Testament passage in which 'an eye for an eye' is contrasted with 'turning the other cheek', tend to think of the *lex talionis* as something primitive and barbaric, almost immoral. While it is primitive, however, it is neither barbaric nor immoral, for it is a primitive way of maintaining public security. In pre-Islamic Arabia there was no sense of a general duty to another man based on the fact that he was a fellow human being. In the abstract there was no fault or sin in killing a man you happened to meet in the desert. You might be restrained from killing him, however, by considerations linked with the system of security and the *lex talionis*; e.g. by the fact that he belonged to an allied tribe towards which your tribe had obligations, or by the fact that he belonged to a strong tribe which would be sure to exact full vengeance. In such ways the *lex talionis* succeeded in restraining wanton killing and injury among the nomads of Arabia.

A presupposition of the effective working of such a system is the solidarity of the kinship group. This means that if a member of the group is killed, the others will at once take steps to avenge him; if he is attacked, they will spring to his support without asking about the rights or wrongs of the matter. It was a sacred duty for each member of the group to give 'help' to another member of the group and, if necessary, to avenge his death. Since there could be no police force in the conditions of the Arabian desert, public security required the highest regard for the duty of revenge and 'help'. Its sacredness and imperative character corresponded to its importance, for, as in societies with a police force, it was essential for the maintenance of law and order that the revenge or punishment should be effectively carried out. For this reason, if the immediate kin of the murdered man were too weak to exact revenge, they could appeal to a wider kinship group or ask the help of a strong tribe. Revenge was also made easier by the solidarity of the kinship group in the sharing of guilt. It would often have been easy for a killer to remain hidden in the vast expanses of the desert with the connivance of his kinsmen; but the whole group was held responsible, and vengeance was satisfied with the blood of one member of the group. Even modern occidental administrators with ideas of individual responsibility have found that the only practicable course in the desert is to hold the whole group responsible.[4]

In societies which follow the *lex talionis* the original demand of an actual life for a life comes in time to be modified by the possibility of accepting blood-money or a blood-wit as an alternative. In Arabia this possibility may have been introduced shortly before the time of Muḥammad. The sacredness attached to the duty of revenge is well illustrated by the fact that the die-hard conservatives or strict moralists taunted those who accepted camels instead of a human life with being content with milk instead of blood. Nevertheless it came to be regarded as respectable to accept camels if the killer and his kinsmen managed to avoid the avengers until the first heat of their anger had died down. In Muḥammad's time the blood-wit for an adult male was a hundred camels and for a woman fifty. Shortly before 1914, when Alois Musil was studying the Rwala tribe in the Syrian desert, the blood-wit for a man of a related tribe was a mare, fifty she-camels and a rider's equipment, and for a woman twenty-five she-camels.[5]

Important features of this system of security are related to the concept of protection. The solidarity of the kinship group meant that the member was protected by the group. The group of close kinsmen, however, might be relatively weak; and if they appealed for help to a wider group of kin, the obligation on the latter was slight, and they might reject an appeal for help without incurring any disgrace. There were various devices, however, which increased the size and strength of the group or extended the circle of those obliged to help it.

First, persons might be attached to the group as clients (*mawālī*; sing. *mawlā*). This might come about in various ways.[6] When a slave was freed he normally became the client of his former master, who was then called his patron (also *mawlā*). A weak person requiring protection might be given the status of client by an exchange of oaths. Again, in early Islamic times, a non-Arab on becoming a Muslim had to be attached as client to an Arab tribe; often it was the tribe of the governor or general before whom he had professed Islam. Secondly, there was the status of 'protected neighbour' (*jār*) conferred on a person who was to be attached to one's tribe for a shorter or longer period. A single person could confer 'neighbourly protection' (*jiwār*) and this would normally be acknowledged and observed by the whole tribe. Thirdly, there might be alliance or federation (*ḥilf, taḥāluf*). This was ostensibly between equals, and might be between several individuals or groups; but sometimes, especially when it was between two of whom one was stronger than the other, an element of superiority and inferiority crept in, and the confederate (*ḥalīf*) was hardly distinguishable from the client.

In all these cases the parties were pledged to help one another against enemies to the best of their abilities. Where they were reckoned equal the obligation was mutual. In other cases, however, where a stronger had undertaken to protect a weaker, it was a matter of honour for the stronger to make good his undertaking. Not to make at least an attempt to defend and avenge those one was bound to protect would be shameful in the extreme; taunts would be constantly repeated in verses and on other public occasions, and it would be difficult to live down the incident. The concept of protection is still alive among the true Bedouin and has many ramifications, though some of the words used are different. Writing of the Arab of the Rwala tribe in the early twentieth century Alois Musil said, 'there is nothing he fears as much as dishonor to his good name and a reflection on his character, or, as he says, the blackening of his face'. If he failed to guard a protégé effectually, the latter would tie a black rag to a long stick and go about proclaiming the failure and saying 'May God blacken his face!'[7]

If we now turn back to look at the second, third and fourth points listed from the Constitution of Medina, we see how closely they are related to the pre-Islamic system. According to the articles summarized in the second point the subdivisions of the community–that is, the more immediate kinship groups –are to be responsible for blood-money and ransoms. In other matters, however, in which the concept of protection is relevant, the solidarity of the whole community is emphasized. They are to act as one in questions of peace and war with the unbelievers, that is, primarily, the pagan Meccans. They are to show solidarity in respecting grants of 'neighbourly protection'. Most revolutionary of all, where one member of the community has committed a crime against another member of the community the kinsmen of the criminal, instead of supporting him according to pre-Islamic custom, are to help to see that he is punished.

The provisions of the Constitution are amplified in some respects by the Qur'ān, especially with regard to vengeance for killing or injury. The system of the *lex talionis* seems to have been working tolerably well; and in any case it was so deeply embedded in the Arab outlook that it would have been difficult to replace it by anything else. This is clearly recognized in 42.41/39: 'if any one avenges himself after wrong done to him (that is, his kin), against such there is no way (of proceeding to stop or punish him)'. The previous verse, however, while admitting the justice of retaliation, has recommended forgiveness and reconciliation. In this context–if we remember the taunt about accepting milk instead of blood–what the Qur'ān recommends is presumably in down-to-earth terms the acceptance of a blood-wit of camels. In another passage (4.92/4), where a believer accidentally kills another believer or a person in alliance with the believers, he is commanded to free a slave who is a Muslim and to pay a blood-wit to the family of the victim; and the family was no doubt required to accept the blood-wit. On the other hand, the believer who kills another believer deliberately is said to be in Hell (4.93/5); and presumably if the family of the victim took vengeance, no questions would be asked. The main effort of Muḥammad as head of state and of later Islamic governments seems to have been to persuade men to accept a blood-wit and to secure agreement about the amount to be paid.

4. The nature of the community

In the Constitution of Medina a special word, *umma*, is used for the 'community', and it is therefore desirable to look more closely at the precise meaning of the word. Some older scholars were attracted by its similarity to the Arabic word for 'mother', *umm*; but it is now generally agreed that the two words are distinct, even if their similarity may have led to a certain connection of thought among Arabic-speakers. The word is almost certainly borrowed from the Hebrew *ummā* meaning 'tribe' or 'people', and that in turn may be borrowed from a Sumerian word.[8] The word *umma* is found in an old Arabic inscription, but otherwise does not seem to have been widely used; at least recent writers on the question have not cited any examples from pre-Islamic poetry. The numerous examples in the Qur'ān have been carefully examined by a modern scholar and the conclusion reached that the word is always applied to certain ethnic, linguistic or 'confessional' communities which are the object of the divine plan of salvation.[9] This conclusion, however, is only to be accepted with some qualifications. A general consideration is that any group of people mentioned in the Qur'ān is likely to be brought into connection with 'the divine plan of salvation', since this is a primary concern of the Qur'ān. It also becomes clear that an *umma* is not necessarily a community of God-fearing people, for there are passages which speak of a whole *umma* or several such rejecting the messenger sent to them and being consigned as a community to Hell; thus 7.38/6 envisages numerous communities in Hell and the latest-arrived *umma* complaining that the others had given it a bad example and should have a double punishment.

Another curious fact is that none of the passages in the Qur'ān with the word *umma* appears to be later than the year 625. There is no obvious explanation for this; it might be because of the growing complexity of the political structure of the body of Muslims and their dependents; or one might conjecture that the Jews of Medina had been making fun of the word in some way. The retention of the word *umma* in the Constitution, provisionally dated 627, can be explained as due to the fact that the articles containing it were repeated from an earlier document. In most of the Qur'ānic instances of the word assigned to the Medinan period there is a definite religious reference. The Muslims constitute an *umma* in the middle (2.143/37); and the Jews and Christians also are communities, though it is not clear whether each is one or several. When the word comes to be used again in later Islamic literature it has a religious connotation.

The common Arabic word for 'tribe' or 'people' is *qawm*. It properly designates a kinship group forming an effective political and social unit, but the number of persons in it varies considerably. The more widely the net of kinship is spread, the less effective is the group or collection of groups as an operative unit. The English words 'tribe' and 'clan' are used in this study to indicate larger and smaller kinship groups, but not in any exact fashion. In the Qur'ān *qawm* occurs much more frequently than *umma*. In some of the early examples there is a distinct religious reference; thus the Meccans who reject Muḥammad are called a 'proud transgressing *qawm*' (52.32), and in a description of a disobedient community destroyed by a whirlwind it is said that 'the *qawm* was seen laid prostrate' (69.7). There are few examples of the word in the very early passages, but it continues to be used after *umma* ceases to be mentioned. It never appears to have acquired a specifically religious connotation, however.

The conclusions to be drawn from this examination of material is that to begin with there was little difference between the two words, *qawm* and *umma*. Both represented a natural group or community. Prophets were thought of as being sent to such natural communities. It is probable that to the contemporaries of Muḥammad the Jews of Medina were not a religious community but a natural (ethnic or linguistic) community or group of such communities. When the Qur'ān speaks of an *umma* from among the People of the Book the word is to be understood in this way. The common assumption among the Arabs of this period was probably that a natural community would all participate in the same religious rites. If there appears to be a change in the meaning of *umma*, this is to be linked with the developing nature of the actual community of Muḥammad's followers and allies and their dependents. Contemporaries probably felt that *umma* was more appropriate than *qawm* to a group with this kind of complexity. In their eyes it would be a federation of kinship groups, and would not be defined by religion. The Qur'ān itself provides evidence that for some time Muḥammad had alliances with non-Muslims, perhaps even with polytheists; e.g. in one of the verses about the paying of blood-wit (4.92/4) the case is mentioned of the believer who belongs to a *qawm* which has a treaty or compact (*mīthāq*) with the believers, and the presumption is that this *qawm* consists mainly of unbelievers, probably polytheists.

It was only natural that Arabs in the early seventh century should have the concept of 'tribe' at the centre of their political thinking. The great majority of Arabs had no experience of any body politic other than the tribe. In Mecca there was a senate or council (*mala'*), but it probably differed little from the tribal council of a sheykh, except that there was no single head of state in Mecca but a number of ostensibly equal clan-chiefs. Beyond this a few of the Meccan merchants had been in contact with Byzantine and Persian provincial administrations and with the Ethiopian court. In the first two cases the contacts were probably of a limited and superficial character, and gave the Meccans little idea of how these governmental institutions worked; and even if they gained some understanding, it would be difficult to convey this to their less widely travelled fellow-Arabs. It is therefore not surprising to find in the biographies of Muḥammad naïve stories about the reactions of the Byzantine emperor to a letter from Muḥammad; the emperor is depicted as acting as one would expect a tribal sheykh to act, calling together his notables to hear about the letter, listening to their protests and then agreeing to what they all wanted although they were acting on the basis of purely personal feelings.[10]

The use of other names like *umma* does not mean that the concept of the tribe and its solidarity had ceased to be central in Arab political thinking. When the word *umma* disappeared from the Qur'ān about 625, no other single word took its place, unless it was the actual word for 'tribe', namely, *qawm*. For the most part the community was simply called 'the believers' (*mu'minūn*). This term, it may be noted in passing, is much commoner in the Qur'ān than 'the Muslims'. The term *jamā'a*, also meaning 'community' but connoting a number of units joined together, is found in some treaty-documents of Muḥammad's time.[11] The need for a specific name for the community was rendered less urgent by the use of phrases such as 'the treasury of God' for the state treasury, and 'the protection of God and of Muḥammad' for the protection afforded by the Islamic state.

The growing complexity during Muḥammad's lifetime of the

body politic which he directed did not make pre-Islamic concepts irrelevant. Indeed the process of growth can be regarded as taking place in accordance with pre-Islamic principles. The clans at Medina, with whom Muḥammad is presumed to have entered into alliance, themselves already had alliances with some of the nomadic Arab tribes in the neighbourhood. Muḥammad's expeditions or razzias of the year 623, though failing to capture any Meccan caravan, may have been successful in enabling him to form alliances with the nomads already in alliance with Medinan clans. At this stage in Muḥammad's career these were perhaps chiefly pacts of non-aggression, since Muḥammad was still too weak to support these tribes against the Meccans and so could not expect them to take part in his fighting against the Meccans. Such tribes were presumably among the unbelievers with whom he had a treaty or compact (*mīthāq*). As his strength grew, however, his terms for alliance became stiffer. This was particularly so after the capture of Mecca and the victory of Ḥunayn in 630. The following period came to be known as 'the Year of Deputations' because nearly all the Arab tribes which had not already become allies sent deputations to Medina requesting alliance.

The result of this diplomatic activity was to create a federation of tribes in alliance with Muḥammad. The sources, if read superficially, suggest that this was a federation of all the tribes in Arabia; but careful examination shows that this was not the case. In some cases the deputation represented not the whole tribe but only a section of it; sometimes it might be a faction which hoped, by gaining Muḥammad's ear first, to get the better of a rival faction in tribal politics. It seems probable too – though this is a matter of inference – that there were at least two types of alliance with Muḥammad. The normal type was where the tribe agreed to become Muslims – to perform the worship (or prayer) and pay the tithe (*zakāt*), as the Qur'ān expresses it. Such an alliance meant that the tribe in question became a part of the Islamic state or body politic. Most tribes in Muḥammad's closing years had no option but to accept an alliance of this kind. The other kind of alliance was made with one or two strong tribes on the borders of the Persian empire in what is now Iraq. With the breakdown of the Persian imperial administration about 628 such tribes were in a position to carry out raids on the settled lands of southern Iraq without any help from Muḥammad. It was important for the Muslims, however, not to become rivals of these tribes in any raids in this region. For a time, then, it appears that a few of these strong tribes were 'independent allies' of Muḥammad, that is, allies on a footing of equality, not members of the Islamic state, and not necessarily Muslims.[12]

Despite this vast growth of the Islamic state it could still be conceived in terms of the pre-Islamic tribe. It was essentially a federation of tribes. Bertram Thomas has called it a 'super-tribe'.[13] The original *umma* of the Constitution of Medina may have been regarded as something special, not entirely covered by pre-Islamic ideas; but if so, this is nowhere clearly stated. The modern scholar is therefore justified in regarding the political structure of the Islamic state as entirely in accordance with pre-Islamic ideas. A little reflection confirms this view. Muḥammad wanted to have a local community or body politic in which he would be free to proclaim his religion and the Muslims would be able to carry out their rites publicly. The men of Medina may also have had other aims, but at least many were Muslims and in favour of having a place where their religion could be practised. Now when Muḥammad and the men of Medina came together to devise a political structure under which Islam could be practised, it would be unnatural for them to devise some completely novel political structure; they would create a structure in terms of the political concepts with which they were familiar. In other words the religious factor was present in the motives leading Muḥammad and the men of Medina to seek an agreement, but the details of the agreement were in terms of pre-Islamic political concepts. The religious factor again produced the decision (whenever it was made) to restrict membership of the community to Muslims; but this was not primarily a decision about structure. The conclusion, then, is that in its origins the Islamic state was based on, and exemplified, pre-Islamic political concepts.

5. The Jihād or 'holy war'

The Jihād or 'holy war' was a fundamental part of the mechanism of Islamic expansion both within Arabia and in the wider world. It cannot be understood, however, except in the whole context of Arab life; and it can easily be misinterpreted if it is conceived in terms of later occidental conceptions. This applies primarily to the first century or so of Islam, for it must be admitted that changes occurred after that and rulers sometimes abused the practice of Jihād.

An important feature of the life of the nomads of the Arabian deserts from before the time of Muḥammad until the coming of the petrol motor in the twentieth century was the raid or razzia. Modern descriptions[14] tally very well with what we know of the early seventh century. The razzia was almost a form of sport, and could be the chief occupation of the leading men of a tribe. The aim was usually to drive off the camels of some other tribe. This other tribe must be an unfriendly or hostile one; it could not be one of those with whom you had an alliance. Normally there was no loss of life, since the usual strategy was to descend on a small group of men with overwhelming force; under such circumstances it was no disgrace for the attacked party to withdraw. If the victims were stronger than expected, there might be fighting, and lives could be lost.

It is not clear how Muḥammad expected the Emigrants from Mecca in 622 to gain a livelihood after they reached Medina. He can hardly have expected them to become peasants or to depend permanently on the hospitality of the Muslims of Medina. Perhaps he envisaged raiding. Certainly the whole history of Muḥammad's ten years at Medina came to be regarded as a series of razzias or 'expeditions'. The first razzias may have been undertaken by the Emigrants alone, perhaps in sheer boredom, and do not seem to have had any religious significance. According to some versions the first expedition in which Medinan Muslims took part was that which included the battle of Badr in 624–Muḥammad's first great victory against the Meccans. The Qur'ān now exhorts all Muslims to take part in the fighting against the Meccans; this is the best way to interpret 5.35/9, 'O believers, fear God . . . and strive in His way'. There are also verses, however, which distinguish the Emigrants from the Medinan Muslims precisely on the grounds that the former are 'those who believed and emigrated and strove with goods and person in the way of God' (8.72/3) or 'those who emigrated after being persecuted and strove and endured (hardships) patiently' (16.110/1). The word for 'strove' here is *jāhadū*, to which corresponds the verbal noun *jihād*, properly 'striving' or 'the expending of effort'.[15]

It would appear, therefore, that as a result of the hostility of the Meccans the Emigrants came to engage in certain activities which were spoken of as *jihād* or 'striving'. To begin with these may have included normal trading operations, but soon the word came to be used exclusively of participating in razzias or expeditions, and this activity was given a religious reference in that it was said to be 'in the way of God'.

This religious reference is to be interpreted in the light of the Arab system of protection. According to the Constitution of Medina the community of Muslims was to show solidarity in its external relations. So far as razzias were concerned, this meant that they could not be directed against members of the community or tribes in alliance with it, but must always be against hostile or unfriendly tribes. As it became usual to speak of the protection afforded by the community as 'the protection of God and his prophet', it was natural that expeditions against those outside that protection should have been said to have been 'in the way of God'. Moreover the community of Muslims grew stronger with each success, and showed itself more able to defend or avenge its members and those under its wing. Thus a razzia might lead to a weak group in the neighbourhood of Medina asking to be taken into 'the protection of God and his prophet'. In this way the Jihād in the way of God might lead to the adoption of Islam by those who had been attacked.

This is the situation that is commonly described by saying that the opponents of Muḥammad were offered a choice between Islam and the sword. As will be seen later, this is inexact and only applied to pagan Arabs; Jews, Christians and members of other religions had a third option (which they normally selected) namely, to become a 'protected community' under the Islamic state. Pagan Arabs, however, did in effect have this choice between Islam and the sword, but it was not so much deliberate policy as something implicit in Arabian conditions. Since, apart from alliances, every tribe was against every other tribe, a tribe had to be either for Muḥammad or against him after his conquest of Mecca; neutrality was impossible when his power could be felt in most parts of Arabia. The decision to be for Muḥammad or against him was basically a political decision. The religious aspect came in because Muḥammad insisted that those who wanted to become his allies must accept him as prophet, and this involved becoming Muslims.

In the concept of protection as applied to the Islamic state some form of expansion was logically involved. If Muḥammad wanted the tribes in alliance with him to forgo raiding one another, there had to be some outward movement. Men accustomed for generations to the razzia could not be stopped all at once. If they could only raid those outside the Islamic state and its alliance, then, as the state expanded, their raids had to go further afield. A case can be made out for thinking that Muḥammad saw this necessity as early as 626. Certainly, though the sources are unusually silent about details, his expeditions along the road to Syria were the largest he undertook apart from those against Mecca itself.[16] It is difficult not to suppose that he realized the possibility and indeed necessity of expanding into Syria. Similarly he seems to have prepared for expansion into Iraq by alliances with the strong tribes along that frontier.

The phenomenal expansion of the Arabs in the century after Muḥammad's death in 632 was a continuation of Muḥammad's policy of Jihād. There was probably no thought of extending religion by conquest. Expansion rather came through further development of the razzia. The energies of the Arab nomads, roused and directed outwards by Muḥammad, continued to move outwards. Booty was the primary aim of most of the participants in the conquests. Expeditions were directed to where booty was plentiful and the opposition not too serious. The significance of the battle of Tours (or Poitiers) in 732 was that it showed the Muslims that further raids into central France would be unprofitable, since the booty to be gained would not be worth the fighting entailed.

The conception of Jihād made a difference to these raiding expeditions which affected the final outcome in important ways. Apart from Islam the tribes of north-east Arabia might have raided Iraq, carried off rich booty, and in a year or two been as poor as ever. As has already been noted, the conception of Jihād modified the practice of raiding for booty by introducing the ever-expanding sphere of protection. Beyond this, however, the leaders of the Islamic state adopted a policy which prevented the results of raiding expeditions from being merely ephemeral. In particular they established an organization which made it possible to conquer and retain land without reducing their fighting strength. The men in the armies were not allowed to settle on the land and had no individual allocations. Instead the rents and taxes of the lands were centrally collected and then divided out among the Muslims, who were all expected to take a share in the expeditions. The peasants or other inhabitants of conquered lands usually accepted the status of a 'protected community', and in this way came within the Islamic state. An advanced base for the army could then be established among them, and from this base raids could be made still further afield. This was the method which enabled the Muslims to advance through North Africa, then into Spain and through Spain into France. (Matters of provincial administration will be considered later.)

From this account of the Jihād it will be seen that the description of 'holy war' is most misleading. The Jihād of the first great expansion is a development of the Arabian razzia–a logical development because of the increasing extension of the *pax islamica*. Most of the participants in the expeditions probably thought of nothing more than booty–movable booty was distributed among them. Some of them were certainly pious Muslims to whom it meant something that they were fighting in the way of God. More of them probably believed that, if they died in the fighting, they would be reckoned martyrs and would go to Paradise. There was no thought of spreading the religion of Islam; apart from other considerations that would have meant sharing their privileges of booty and stipends with many neo-Muslims. It doubtless increased their self-esteem that the 'strong tribe' of Muslims should take under its protection the 'weak tribes' of Jews and Christians. The most that can be said at the level of the individual is that religious and materialistic motives support one another. At the level of the high command, however, the religious idea of the solidarity of all believers and its corollary of the necessity of directing warlike energies outwards led to the building of an empire. Muḥammad cannot have foreseen the expansion in detail, but the fact that at his death, when the situation in Medina was threatening, Abū-Bakr did not cancel an expedition towards Syria, suggests that Muḥammad had impressed on his lieutenants the centrality of the need for movement outwards.

After the first century or so of the Islamic state the character of the Jihād changed, and indeed it was only heard of from time to time. The system by which all able-bodied Muslims served in the army was abandoned. There were by this time too many Muslims and also great reluctance to serve. By the early ninth century the ʿAbbāsid caliphs were finding it more effective to have mercenaries, especially for the maintenance of internal order. There was now little point in speaking of a 'holy war'. For a great empire, too, the conception of Jihād – implying war, where likely to be successful, against all those of another religion – was not a satisfactory basis for foreign policy. The conception of Jihād was of course frequently invoked by later politicians, sometimes justifiably (as in the case of frontier wars against non-Muslims), sometimes unjustifiably. It was easy to rouse the populace to fight against one's enemies by calling them infidels and proclaiming a Jihād. The Ottoman Sultan proclaimed a Jihād in 1914 when he declared war against Great Britain, because he hoped that the Muslims of India would support him against the British. Unfortunately for him the Muslims were not too dissatisfied with the British, and moreover had observed that the Ottoman Sultan was prepared to be junior partner in an alliance with other infidels. Another useful device was to proclaim some new views as the true Islam, and then on this basis denounce as unbelievers the people one wanted to attack.

Thus the conception of Jihād was chiefly important during Muḥammad's lifetime and in the century afterwards. At later times the best that can be said of it is that it has roused ordinary men to military activity. Some mystics asserted that 'the greater Jihād' was inner self-discipline.

TWO

MUḤAMMAD AS HEAD OF STATE

1. Muḥammad's position under the Constitution

Just as the Islamic community or state has been found to be based on pre-Islamic ideas from the Arabian nomads, so one might expect Muḥammad's position in the community to have a similar basis. This is indeed the case, but Muḥammad is more than a chief of a tribe or even the leader of a federation of tribes.

In pre-Islamic Arabia the functions of leadership were not concentrated in the hands of one man. There was indeed a head or *sayyid* for each tribe (in later times also called 'sheykh, *shaykh*), but his authority was limited. He presided as *primus inter pares* at councils of the notables of the tribe, and, in so far as he was respected, what he said was listened to attentively; only a man who was himself of some weight would venture to differ. The *sayyid* usually made the final decisions about moving pasture, and conducted negotiations with other tribes. He was not necessarily the leader in war, however, for this function was often in the hands of another person known as the *qā'id*; nor was he responsible for the administration of justice, except in so far as judicial matters came before the council of notables. Difficult judgements were normally brought before a special person known as a *ḥakam* or 'arbiter'. In each region of Arabia a few men, noted for their tact, wisdom and knowledge of ancestral custom, were widely accepted as arbiters. Such men had no executive powers, but, if a case was brought before one of them, he would try to ensure that his judgement would be carried out, by requiring beforehand that each party should take a solemn oath to perform his decision and should hand over a number of camels to a neutral person.

When with these points in mind the Constitution of Medina is examined, it will be found that Muḥammad is far from being chief of the *umma* or Islamic community. Very little, indeed, is said about his position. In the preamble he is spoken of as 'the Messenger of God', and there are two articles (§23, 42) stating that disputes within the community are to be referred 'to God and to Muḥammad'. Otherwise there is nothing. It may be assumed, however, that he was regarded as chief or *sayyid* of the Emigrants; but they only count as one clan among nine. Apart from being the Messenger of God, Muḥammad was not superior to the other clan chiefs.

The articles about referring disputes to Muḥammad are to be understood in the first place as making him a kind of arbiter. Shortly before his Hijra to Medina in 622 there had been a battle with much bloodshed. Most of the clans of Medina had joined one side or the other, roughly according to a genealogical division into two tribes (the Aws and the Khazraj); and the resulting blood-wits had not been agreed on so that there was no real peace in the oasis. Many of the Medinans probably hoped that Muḥammad would help to make and keep peace. For the work of an arbiter, too, his prophethood was an advantage, since it suggested that he was a man of superior wisdom. The phrase about the referring of disputes 'to God and to Muḥammad' may mean that decisions were to be based on the word of God in the Qur'ān where applicable; or it may merely mean that Muḥammad would be given divine help in his decisions. In either case the religious aura surrounding Muḥammad enhanced his suitability to perform the function of an arbiter.

Muḥammad's comparative weakness in the first few years at Medina can be illustrated by one or two incidents. One such is 'the affair of the Lie' which involved his young and favourite wife 'Ā'isha, daughter of his chief lieutenant Abū-Bakr. She had accompanied Muḥammad on an expedition (in 627 or 628) but on the last halt on the way home had been left behind unnoticed and then later had arrived in Medina on the camel of a handsome young man. At this tongues wagged. The gossip was seized on by Muḥammad's bitterest opponent in Medina in order to discredit him and perhaps to disrupt his relations with Abū-Bakr. Eventually when a Qur'ānic passage was revealed pronouncing 'Ā'isha blameless and it was clear that she was not pregnant, Muḥammad decided to teach a lesson to the mischief-makers. He had no authority to punish, however. Instead he had to call a meeting of all the heads of clans and ask for pressure to be placed–that is, by their own clans–on those slandering his family. This 'show-down' made clear the opponents' weakness and lack of support among the people of Medina, but it also illustrates for us Muḥammad's far-from-autocratic position. Similarly in 627, when he wanted to punish the Jewish clan of Qurayẓa which had intrigued with the enemy during the siege of Medina, he could not proceed directly, but had to ask the leader of their confederate clan to pronounce sentence. In these early years it is also probable that many disputes were not referred to Muḥammad, since there are several verses in the Qur'ān exhorting the Muslims to make such referrals to God and to Muḥammad, or criticizing some of them for not doing so.[1]

With regard to the position of military leader, on the other hand, there seems to have been no dispute. The descriptions of the expeditions make it clear that he came to be accepted as leader by the whole community. There is no explicit statement how this came about, but reading between the lines we reach some such account as the following. The earliest expeditions were raids of the 'clan' of Emigrants–'striving in the way of God' was an activity distinguishing them from the Muslims of Medina–and for these expeditions the Emigrants accepted Muḥammad as leader, at least in name, even when he did not take part in person. Subsequently, either through personal invitation or because encouraged to do so by the Qur'ān, the Medinan Muslims joined in Muḥammad's expeditions. Since he and the Emigrants were the entrepreneurs, as it were, of the expeditions, the command was naturally left in his hands. Especially after the prestige of his victory at Badr in 624 nobody was likely to suggest that any other should lead the Muslims in battle. Later expeditions, if not led by Muḥammad himself, were under the command of a man designated by him. In this way without any difficulty Muḥammad received the office of *qā'id* or war-leader. The Qur'ān further enjoined the payment to him of a fifth of the proceeds of all expeditions formally sponsored by Muḥammad and the Islamic state.[2] This was comparable to the 'quarter' traditionally given to the chief of a tribe after a razzia, and intended to be used for communal purposes. Since the Qur'ān also prescribed the uses to which the 'fifth' was to be put (which were communal), the Islamic rule is a slight modification of an old practice.

2. Muḥammad's position in the later Medinan period

There is no clear record of any formal change in Muḥammad's position in the Islamic state. A possible exception to this is the Pledge of Good Pleasure, but the accounts of this in the sources do not make clear its constitutional effect. At a critical point in the negotiations which led to the treaty of al-Ḥudaybiya between Muḥammad and the Meccans in 628, when it looked as if the Meccans might attack the Muslims, Muḥammad called his followers together under a tree and made them take a pledge to himself. A few versions say it was a pledge to fight to the death for him, but the most widely held account denies this and says it was a pledge not to flee. Yet another source, however, speaks of a pledge to do whatever Muḥammad decided; and this is attractive to the modern scholar, since it is easy to see how this general pledge could have been made more particular as the story was repeated.[3] The name Pledge of Good Pleasure comes from the Qur'ānic verse, 'God was well-pleased with the believers when they pledged themselves to thee (Muḥammad) under the tree' (48.18). Even if it is a pledge to accept Muḥammad's decision, however, it must be interpreted carefully within the whole historical context, and too much weight must not be laid on a single incident.

An important part of the context is that the words 'obey God and his Messenger' or an equivalent occur some forty times in the Qur'ān, and that the majority of these instances can be dated about the year 625. In most cases the command is quite general, and it is sometimes indicated that disobedience will lead to Hell. Such teaching is confirmed by stories of earlier prophets. In a few cases, however, there is a particular reference in the passage, and this may be to some moral point such as the avoidance of wine-drinking. The most important particular complaint, however, is that certain people are not 'obeying God and his Messenger' in respect of the policy of war against Mecca.[4] The policy of war, however, was not a private decision of Muḥammad's but had been prescribed in the Qur'ān. Thus our interpretation of the phrase 'obey God and his Messenger' is not that the Muslims were expected to obey all Muḥammad's decisions but that it refers to the carrying out of Qur'ānic prescriptions, including such decisions of Muḥammad's as were necessary to implement what was prescribed. There is a verse (33.36) denouncing those who reject 'what God and the Messenger have decided' (*qaḍā*), but this refers to decisions of a judicial character, presumably made by Muḥammad in his function of *ḥakam* or arbiter.

The increase in Muḥammad's power and authority came about not through any new constitutional agreement but as a result of his military victories and the series of successful expeditions. Many nomadic tribes, on seeing his successes, were ready to enter into friendly agreements with him. Members of some relatively weak tribes actually came to live in Medina and were given the status of 'emigrant'. These were presumably also added to Muḥammad's 'clan' of Emigrants, so that it became the most powerful in Medina. This added to Muḥammad's authority in discussions with nominally equal chiefs of other clans. Some tribes or individuals were given the status of 'emigrants' without actually 'emigrating' or 'making the Hijra' to Medina. In later times this status was important because with it a man received a higher stipend from the public treasury. Even in Muḥammad's lifetime, however, it may have indicated a special relationship to himself.[5]

Along with the external successes went the growth of the system of alliances, and this also strengthened Muḥammad's position. In some cases a tribe or clan might have an alliance with Muḥammad as an individual.[6] Perhaps this was normal in the first five or seven years at Medina. In so far as his alliances became more numerous, Muḥammad's position was strengthened over against the clan chiefs – though they also had alliances. In several of the documents from the later years, on the other hand, there is no mention of alliance, but the document takes the form of a declaration by Muḥammad that, if certain conditions are fulfilled (such as worship, tithe and obedience to Muḥammad) the clan or tribe in question has the protection of God and his Messenger.[7] The fact that such documents take the form of a declaration by Muḥammad shows that by this time he had unquestioned authority in such matters; but the caution should be added that these declarations were probably regarded as belonging to the special sphere of the Messenger.

Even so every increase in the number of groups to which these declarations were made must have enhanced Muḥammad's position. It was presumably in view of Muḥammad's position at the centre of the alliance or federation that he sent out administrators and collectors of tithes to a great many tribes.[8]

Two incidents connected with the expedition to Tabūk in the last three months of 630 illustrate Muḥammad's handling of details of administration. This was the greatest of all Muḥammad's expeditions, both in distance covered and in number of participants–about 30,000. To raise a force of this size Muḥammad had to insist that every able-bodied Muslim should take part. On his return those who had remained at home were examined. Three whose excuses were adjudged insufficient were 'sent to Coventry' by the whole community. The order for this punishment was Muḥammad's own, though presumably regarded as the implementation of a Qur'ānic command; but the termination of the punishment after fifty days was attributed to God through a Qur'ānic revelation (probably 9.118/9).[9]

The second incident was linked with more serious intrigues against Muḥammad. Before he set out for Tabūk he was invited to pray in a new mosque which some Muslims had built in the southern part of the oasis, perhaps five kilometres from the main mosque. He postponed his visit until after his return. On the expedition he heard of a plot against his life; some one was to stumble against him on a rough stretch of road on a dark night and to make the injury look like an accident. Muḥammad must have had some information connecting this plot with the mosque-builders. He had also heard that the latter were hoping to use the mosque as a convenient meeting-place to hatch further plots. He was apparently not in a position, however, to proceed overtly against the plotters, and instead sent two men by night to destroy the mosque. This settled the matter, for no complaints were made. About the same time a Qur'ānic revelation had excommunicated those disaffected Muslims known as 'hypocrites', and this probably applied to some of the mosque-builders.[10]

If we now turn back to consider the interpretation of the Pledge of Good Pleasure, it is clear that it did not by itself create a new constitutional position. In the internal affairs of the community at Medina any autocratic measures would have been abhorrent to the Arabs and would have provoked serious opposition. The Pledge may indeed have been limited to acceptance of Muḥammad's decisions in respect of the particular expedition. Yet, even if it were so limited, it set a precedent. From this time onwards Muḥammad more and more makes the decisions himself in matters that belong to the sphere of the Messenger, that is, especially in the implementation of Qur'ānic commands. Such commands, of course, might deal with matters which a modern occidental would call political and secular. Yet the Muslims of Medina must have had a sufficiently clear idea of what belonged to the sphere of the Messenger. There were many civil and secular affairs which did not belong to this sphere except when Muḥammad was brought in as arbiter; and he seems to have been careful not to give any grounds for thinking he was trying to interfere here. Nevertheless the attractiveness of his personality, the strength of the support he had in Medina itself, and his central place in a vast alliance combined to give him such authority that none was likely to question his delimitation of the sphere of the Messenger. In the external affairs of the Islamic state he was thus virtually an autocrat.

3. The political relevance of religion

It is difficult for the average European or American reader of a biography of Muḥammad not to feel that there is something wrong, even evil, about his position as a head of state. The basic assumption of these readers is well expressed by Frants Buhl, whose life of Muḥammad (published in Danish in 1903 and in German in 1930) is still accepted as one of the standard accounts, when he began a sentence, 'In the case of a purely spiritual movement such as that brought into being by Muḥammad ...'[11] Yet as the horizons of historians widen to include all recorded history in every continent and every century, as in the work of Arnold Toynbee, it becomes clear that the recent occidental conception of 'a purely spiritual movement' is exceptional. Throughout most of human history religion has been intimately involved in the whole life of man in society, and not least in his politics. Even the purely religious teaching of Jesus–as it is commonly regarded–is not without its political relevance. The Gospels constantly have in the background an awareness of the fact that Palestine has been incorporated in the Roman empire and that some contemporary Jewish attitudes will lead to the military destruction of the Jewish people (as in fact happened). If the nascent Christian movement adopted political quietism, this was not because of a permanent separation of religion and politics, but because such a course was *political* wisdom in the circumstances of that particular time and place.

In the case of Islam, though Muḥammad had no political power for the first ten or twelve years of his preaching, there was no sudden change in his outlook when he went to Medina in 622 and gradually began to acquire power. From the first the religious message proclaimed by Muḥammad had been addressed to a *qawm* or *umma*, a 'tribe' or 'community', that is, to a body politic of the type familiar to the Arabs. When Muḥammad was accused of political aspirations, the Qur'ān instructed him to reply that he was only a 'warner'; but this warning was a warning to the whole community that such false attitudes as niggardliness and pride in their own power would lead to catastrophe, and in order to correct such attitudes something approaching political activity would be necessary. The Qur'ānic phrase (88.22) that Muḥammad is not a 'controller' (= 'overseer' – *muṣayṭir*) over the Meccans may reflect the feeling among some of them that he was in danger of becoming so because he had access to a superhuman source of knowledge about what was good or bad for the community. This would indicate that the political relevance of his preaching was felt even by his opponents.

It is worth noting at this point that, although in European languages Muḥammad is usually called 'prophet', his normal appellation in Arabic is *rasūl Allāh*, 'the Messenger of God', or 'the one sent by God'. The Qur'ān uses both terms and speaks of Muḥammad as one among numerous prophets and even more numerous messengers. While Muḥammad is at first regarded in the Qur'ān simply as the bearer of a message to men, in particular a message of 'warning', in the Medinan period the term *rasūl* may have come to mean 'one commissioned to do something', and this may be something of a practical character, such as managing some of the affairs of Medina, as well as conveying a message. Thus the term 'Messenger of God' in contrast to 'Prophet' may indicate that the practical and political activity in which Muḥammad engaged was commissioned by God.

If we look more generally at the relation between religion and politics, it is helpful to consider first the place of religion in the life of an individual. In the case of a person to whom religion means something and is not a merely nominal adherence, two points may be emphasized. First, the ideas of his religion constitute the intellectual framework within which he sees all his activity taking place. It is from this relationship to a wider context that his activities gain their significance, and a consideration of this relationship may influence his general plan for his life in particular ways. Secondly, because religion brings an awareness of this wider context in which the possible aims for a man's life are set, it may often generate the motives for his activity; indeed, without the motives given by religion some activities cannot be carried out. From these two points it is seen that religion has a central position in a man's life, not because it determines many of the details (though in some cases it may), but because it gives him general aims in life and helps to concentrate his energies in the pursuit of these aims.

Where religion is conceived in an individualistic fashion, that is, where apart from ritual and worship it is chiefly concerned with matters of individual morality, it will have little relevance to politics. If some of its prescriptions of individual morality conflict with the moral ideas generally accepted in the community and enforced by the state–e.g. if the religion says that bearing arms as a soldier is sinful–there is a possibility of conflict. Such points will tend to be peripheral, even though the feelings provoked may be bitter. The situation is completely different, however, where the outlook of the religion is communalistic. In Islam communal solidarity has always had a prominent place, and this is still so at the present day. Islam has from the first been relevant to the political and social organization of the community. It is true that in its beginnings there was some emphasis on the fact that man's assignment to Paradise or Hell for eternity was on an individualistic basis; but (as will be seen later) in course of time the general view of Muslims was that no one who maintained intact his membership of the community of Islam would be eternally in Hell.

Because of this emphasis on communal solidarity and because of the circumstances of its origin–the wielding of political power by Muḥammad–there has never in Islam been any contrast comparable to that in Christianity between 'the church' and 'the world'. The normal community has always been a solidly Muslim community. Even when there were non-Muslims in it, they had to live as separate groups largely isolated from the main community. It also follows that for Islam there is less distinction between the religious and the secular. There is indeed an Arabic phrase (*dīnī wa-dunyawī*) which is commonly translated 'religious and secular' but which properly means 'religious and this-worldly'. Moreover the connotations of the Arabic word *dīn* in Islamic countries, though it may be translated 'religion', are quite different from those of the English word 'religion'. *Dīn* may cover nearly the whole conduct of life.

It may be argued further and with a measure of truth that religions, strictly speaking, have no political concepts attached to them. What is found is that a religion sometimes favours the political concepts of the region of its origin. This certainly is the case with Islam. Among the nomadic tribes of Arabia there was as great a degree of communal solidarity as anywhere else in the world. In Mecca before the preaching of Muḥammad commercial prosperity was breaking down the solidarity of tribe and clan. Islam may be said to have restored communal solidarity but to have attached it to the total community of Muslims rather than to any smaller unit. Much of the growth of Islam in tropical Africa in the last hundred years may be traced to its preservation of this sense of communal solidarity.

It is indeed the solidarity of the *umma* or community which is the chief contribution of the Islamic religion in the political sphere. Other political concepts, which were derived from the nomadic tribe, proved unsuitable to a large empire or even to a large, partly urbanized state. Thus despite the fact that Islam has the reputation of being a political religion, it has been relatively unsuccessful in the political field.[12] Some of its first concepts have been abandoned. Where it has achieved satisfactory and durable political arrangements this has often been due to the introduction of new concepts derived from regions which it has conquered. Examples of this are the Persian forms of imperial administration, and the Ottoman slave-household.

These points will become clearer, it is hoped, as this study progresses.

While the fostering of the solidarity of the community may be said to be due to the essence of the Islamic religion, a religion may also have political effects which are of an accidental or incidental nature. Thus the pilgrimage to Mecca, besides its purely religious purposes, must always have helped Muslims to realize more fully the solidarity of the community. In recent times, however, with the greater ease of communication from all parts of the world, the pilgrimage has encouraged friendly relationships between Muslims from different states, and contributed to the potential political unity of the Islamic world. Similarly a modern government might conceivably use for political purposes the sermon at the midday worship or prayer on Fridays. This is the one occasion in the week when all adult male Muslims are expected to go to the central mosque of their town, and when a sermon or address is the norm. Traditionally the address is formal and stylized; but a modern statesman who believed his policies were in accordance with the Sharīʿa could doubtless influence the preachers and use the Friday sermon to promote his political ends.[13] King (ʿAbd-al ʿAzīz) Ibn-Saʿūd is said to have used the address during the pilgrimage in some such way.

THREE

THE EARLY CALIPHATE

1. The situation at Muḥammad's death

Muḥammad died on 8 June 632 after less than a fortnight's illness. There is no evidence that he had seriously considered what arrangements should be made for the government of the state after his death. Perhaps he had thought about the matter and even talked it over with Abū-Bakr and ʿUmar; but, if so, he must have concluded that it was best for him not to try to impose any solution. The normal Arab practice was for the tribal council to meet after the death of a chief, and any attempt to limit beforehand the choice of the council might have been resented. Had Muḥammad's adoptive son, Zayd ibn-Ḥāritha, been alive, he might have succeeded without difficulty; but he had been killed in fighting. Muḥammad's cousin and son-in-law ʿAlī ibn-Abī-Ṭālib, though great claims have been made for him by the Shīʿites, must have been unacceptable to many Muslims.

At the end death came suddenly, and ʿUmar is credited with having tried to conceal it. Abū-Bakr, who happened to be in a distant part of the town, was hastily summoned, and made the famous announcement, 'If any one worships Muḥammad, Muḥammad has died; but if any one worships God, God is living and does not die'. The Muslims of Medina (the Anṣār) quickly called a meeting and were proposing to make their leader Saʿd ibn-ʿUbāda head of the community. Abū-Bakr and ʿUmar proceeded to the hall where the meeting was taking place and were allowed to speak. They argued the need for preserving the whole community as a unity and the improbability of this being achieved if one of the Medinans was appointed, since many nomads were unwilling to accept any leader except a Meccan (that is, of the tribe of Quraysh). The Medinans were themselves divided into two tribes, and those who belonged to the other tribe from Saʿd's began to realize that they might be at a disadvantage. In the end all agreed to accept Abū-Bakr.

There was much to be said for this decision. Abū-Bakr was the most experienced person available, since for over ten years he had been Muḥammad's chief adviser. He had a specially good knowledge of the genealogies – including the intrigues – of the nomadic tribes. His daughter ʿĀ'isha was Muḥammad's chief wife, and this cemented the relationship between the two men. In addition Muḥammad had appointed Abū-Bakr to lead the public worship when his last illness prevented him from doing this himself.

Abū-Bakr is generally held to have taken the title of *khalīfat rasūl Allāh*, 'the caliph of the Messenger of God'. Since this word *khalīfa* or 'caliph' has a long and important history in the Islamic world, it is worth considering what it originally signified. The form *khalīfa* occurs twice in the Qur'ān, and there are seven occurrences in all of two plural forms. There was much discussion among commentators on the Qur'ān about the precise meaning of some of these passages, but no agreed conclusion was reached. It is thus unlikely that the Qur'ān was the source from which Abū-Bakr derived this title. It must come rather from the ordinary secular use of the word.

The difficulty experienced by the commentators arises from the fact that the root of *khalīfa* has had a rich and varied semantic development in Arabic. The meaning of *khalīfa* has so many facets that it is hard to know which is dominant in certain contexts. The basic meaning is 'successor' or, as one commentator defined it, 'one who takes the place of another after him in some matter'.[1] The plural instances in the Qur'ān refer to peoples or tribes who occupy lands formerly occupied by other peoples who have been destroyed by God in punishment for disobedience. In all these cases the translation 'successors' would be justified; but in some of them there is no mention of the predecessors and so little emphasis on succession that the translation 'inhabitants' or 'settlers' would not be seriously misleading.[2] In the singular, however, *khalīfa*, besides meaning 'successor', may also have the suggestion of one who exercises authority, though possibly in a subordinate position. A professor of Qur'ānic textual studies in the early tenth century is said to have had eighty-four assistants who deputized for him in minor matters, and each of these was called a *khalīfa.*[3] It is also a well-known fact that the Mahdī of the Sudan at the end of the nineteenth century planned to appoint four Khalīfas or lieutenants, and one of these eventually succeeded him. Thus a *khalīfa* may be not simply a *de facto* successor, nor only the successor to a position of authority, but also someone who is definitely appointed as a deputy and given the authority or some of the authority of the person appointing him. The commonest translation of *khalīfa* in the dictionaries is 'deputy' or 'viceregent'. An inscription from South Arabia (in a language cognate with classical Arabic) shows that the corresponding word was there used about AD 543 in the sense of 'viceroy'[4] and this usage may have affected that in classical Arabic, especially when the caliphs came to have great political power.

Since Abū-Bakr was not appointed by Muḥammad except to deputize for him in leading the public prayers, the phrase '*khalīfa* of the Messenger of God' cannot have meant 'deputy'. The primary meaning must have been merely 'successor', except that there would be a suggestion of 'one succeeding in the exercise of authority'. Thus the word *khalīfa* as applied to Abū-Bakr was vague; but this vagueness was an asset, since the meaning of the word was able to develop as the office itself grew in importance and changed its character.

There is some evidence to show that no more than thirty years after Muḥammad's death the Umayyad caliphs began to place a new interpretation on the word in order to exalt their office. They allowed the use of the title 'caliph of God' in the sense of ruler or viceroy appointed by God.[5] They further justified their claims to be divinely appointed by quoting the Qur'ānic verse in which God addresses David saying, 'O David, we have made thee a *khalīfa* in the earth; so judge between the people with truth' (38.26/5). From the other verse in which the word *khalīfa* occurs (2.30/28), where God says to the angels, 'I am placing (or making) in the earth a *khalīfa*', namely Adam, it was inferred that the office of *khalīfa* was higher than that of angels and prophets. Some of the opponents of the Umayyads tried to counter the effect of such interpretations by circulating a story according to which Abū-Bakr modestly refused the title of 'caliph of God' and said he was content to be called 'caliph of the Messenger of God'. Despite this story the title 'caliph of God' is still used occasionally of the 'Abbāsids, though mainly in adulatory verse.

If the 'Abbāsids usually avoided an official use of the title 'caliph of God', they were not averse to other titles suggesting that they were divinely appointed or commissioned. One of the best-known is 'shadow of God on the earth', which apparently means that they are the effective agents of God's protection.[6] It is commonly stated that the second caliph, 'Umar I, used the title 'caliph of the caliph of the Messenger of God'. By the time of the third caliph a continuation of this formula would have been too clumsy, and, apart from attempts to use 'the caliph of God', the form was 'caliph of the Messenger of God' or simply 'caliph'. 'Umar I also introduced the title of *amīr al-mu'minīn*, often translated 'commander of the faithful' but sometimes 'prince of the believers'. This may have been felt to give the office of caliph a divine sanction because of the Qur'ānic verse (4.59/62): 'obey God and obey the Messenger and the holders of command (*amr*) among you'. It came to be exclusively used as the protocollary title of the caliphs.[7]

It will be convenient here to mention some of the later uses of the title of caliph, though the changes in the character of the supreme office in the Islamic world will be described later. In 909 the Shī'ite dynasty of the Fāṭimids established a kingdom in Tunisia, and, because they claimed to be rightful rulers of the whole Islamic world, took the titles of 'caliph' and 'commander of the faithful'. The Umayyad dynasty of Spain, unwilling that serious rivals like the Fāṭimids should have this appearance of superior status, themselves also adopted these titles, though without claiming to be rulers of the Islamic world. Before the dissolution of the 'Abbāsid caliphate of Baghdad by the Mongols in 1258, many independent Muslim rulers used the title of 'caliph', though some of them were insignificant. After 1258 a series of descendants of the 'Abbāsids lived in Cairo and had the title of 'caliph', though they had virtually no powers and were not generally recognized. Their chief importance is that they enabled later Ottoman sultans to claim that after the Ottoman conquest of Egypt in the sixteenth century these 'Abbāsids had transferred their caliphate to the Ottomans. It continued in the Ottoman dynasty until 1924 when it was abolished by the Turkish republic. The title of 'caliph' has also been used by the successors of the founders of religious and semi-religious movements, like the Sudanese Mahdiyya and the recent Indo-Pak sect of Ahmadiyya.

2. The succession to the caliphate

Succession to the leadership of a nomadic Arab tribe had to take account of the fact that the continued existence of a tribe might depend on it having effective leadership. When a chief died, therefore, he was normally succeeded by the best qualified person in a certain family. The decision was made by a meeting of the adult males of the family or tribe. It was a common idea among the Arabs that noble qualities were inherent in certain stocks and were genetically transmitted. It was presumably for this reason that leadership was restricted to families which had given evidence that their stock carried qualities of leadership. There was no law of primogeniture. Even in ordinary matters of inheritance the first-born had no special privileges. It must have been difficult to determine relative ages in the conditions of pre-Islamic Arabia, especially where matrilineal kinship counted most. After the coming of Islam the problem was continued by the practice of polygamy. This aspect of the Arabian background must be emphasized since it explains the perpetual problem of succession faced by most Islamic dynasties.

What may be called the standard account of the accession of the next three caliphs is as follows. Abū-Bakr, while on his death-bed, designated 'Umar I ('Umar ibn-al-Khaṭṭāb) as his successor in a written document. This designation, however, was preceded by an informal consultation with a few of the leading men, and was followed by the acclamation (*bay'a*), or swearing of allegiance, of the people as a whole. This happened while Abū-Bakr was still alive. 'Umar died after being stabbed by a madman, and had little time to make any plans. He is said to have wanted to designate one of his colleagues, but the latter refused. He therefore appointed a council or *shūrā* to decide on his successor. This council was composed of the six leading men, from among whom the new caliph was bound to be chosen. There are differing accounts of the meetings of the council, and the details probably reflect the feelings of later generations. There is no doubt, however, about the result, namely, the election of ʿUthmān, a member of the family of Umayya, though not reckoned a member of the Umayyad dynasty. It is sometimes stated that ʿUthmān was chosen by the council because he was weak and likely to leave more power in the hands of the others; but this is not certain. He may well have been the most competent statesman, for the clan of Umayya had included some of the best business men in Mecca, and ʿUthmān may have inherited the family talent. The decision of the council was declared in the Mosque and homage was done to ʿUthmān.

During the reign of ʿUthmān (644-56) tensions which had not been felt in the excitement of the expansion under ʿUmar increased and broke into the open. These were perhaps due more to the general situation than to any lack of ability on the part of ʿUthmān. Be that as it may, malcontents besieged him in his house in Medina, and, although he was the ruler of vast territories, he had no troops present in Medina, not even a handful of men as a bodyguard. The leading men of Medina gave some token support, but that was all. After several days the insurgents forced an entrance into his house and killed him. Muḥammad's cousin and son-in-law ʿAlī ibn-Abī-Ṭālib, who had been passed over when ʿUthmān was elected, was the most respected Muslim in Medina, and was acclaimed as caliph in the Mosque by such Muslims as were present in the city.

In appointing ʿUmar, Abū-Bakr had said he was 'the best among the Muslims', and it could be said that in Medina in 656 ʿAlī was so clearly best that no consultation was needed, while ʿUthmān himself had not been in a position to designate anyone as successor.

Such is the standard account of the attainment of the position of caliph by the first four successors of Muḥammad. The four are known as the 'rightly-guided' (*rāshidūn*), and the period covered by their reigns has a special standing in the eyes of Sunnite Muslims. This period is regarded as the ideal or golden age of the caliphate, and because of this has a normative character. Consequently there has been a tendency for each age and body of Muslims to rewrite the history of this period so as to incorporate their own ideals. It is hardly an exaggeration to say that Muslims normally express political theory in the form of history. Perhaps this is to be explained by the deep-rooted Arab conviction that safety is to be found in following exactly the ways of the ancestors. In the case of the rightly-guided caliphs the standard account of their accession given above has been questioned by some modern occidental scholars, but there is no consensus on the matter. In any case a study of the political ideas of the Muslims is bound to concern itself with this standard account, since the elements mentioned in it – taking counsel, designation and acclamation – are widely held to be desirable.

For the period from the death of ʿAlī until the year 750 the caliphate was held by members of the old Meccan clan of Umayya; they are known collectively as the Umayyad dynasty, and had their capital not in Medina but in Damascus. For about ten years up to 692 there was a rival caliph in Mecca in the person of ʿAbd-Allāh ibn-az-Zubayr, but this fact may be neglected here. The interest of the present study is in the new form of succession practised by the Umayyads.

The first Umayyad, Muʿāwiya I, was effective ruler by force of arms of part of the lands of the Muslims before he put forward his claim to be caliph. (Similarly the claim of ʿAbd-Allāh ibn-az-Zubayr was made after he was *de facto* ruler of Mecca.) After the murder of ʿUthmān in 656 Muʿāwiya, who had been governor of Syria for some twenty years, refused to acknowledge ʿAlī as caliph; and thus ʿAlī was never universally recognized by all Muslims. Muʿāwiya did not himself at this point claim the caliphate, but his refusal to acknowledge ʿAlī led to a military confrontation in the region between Syria and Iraq. Before there was serious bloodshed it was agreed to submit the dispute between the two men and the question of the caliphate to two arbiters, one appointed by each side. The Arbitration which followed is the most confused series of events in the whole of Islamic history owing to the way in which the sequence of events and the motives of the participants were altered in the retelling by interested parties.[8] At one point the arbiters almost certainly made a decision unfavourable to ʿAlī, and he refused to accept it. More fighting would probably have taken place, but in January 661 ʿAlī was assassinated.

Already, however, about the middle of 660 Muʿāwiya had had himself proclaimed caliph in Jerusalem. The Umayyads always held that this was based on the award of the arbiters. The accounts of the Arbitration itself are not very helpful, but the arguments used by later Umayyad propaganda are known. The arbiters may have given some weight to the general claim that Muʿāwiya was the person best fitted for the office in view of his long experience. The basic Umayyad claim, however, was that Muʿāwiya acted as heir and avenger of blood for his fellow-clansman ʿUthmān. This claim was strengthened by the fact that some of those responsible for the murder of the caliph were supporters of ʿAlī and he refused to take action against them. According to Arab ideas this gave Muʿāwiya a measure of right. The leaders of the rising against ʿAlī which he defeated at the Battle of the Camel in 656 had also claimed that they were avenging ʿUthmān, though they were more distantly related than Muʿāwiya.

After the death of ʿAlī Muʿāwiya gradually extended his control over all the lands occupied by Muslims, and as he did so he was acknowledged as caliph. While a critic might argue that the Umayyad caliphate inaugurated by Muʿāwiya thus rested on seizure of power by armed force, it had in Arab eyes an appearance of legitimacy. Two of the elements validating the accession of the 'rightly-guided' caliphs were present in Muʿāwiya's case—the taking of counsel (in the form of the Arbitration) and the homage of the people, first in Jerusalem and then elsewhere. The decision of the arbiters, too, must be presumed to have been in accordance with Arab ideas, namely, the recognition as heir of the kinsman ready to act as avenger of blood. To justify their rule the Umayyads also used other arguments which would appeal to Arabs. They claimed that they belonged to the family or clan of the Messenger by speaking of the clan of ʿAbd-Manāf, which included both Umayya and Hāshim as sub-clans (since ʿAbd-Manāf was father of Hāshim and grandfather of Umayya); thus they might be said to have by heredity a share in the qualities of leadership manifested in Muḥammad. They also argued that, since the caliphate had been bestowed on them by God, to disobey the caliph or his subordinates was tantamount to disobeying God; and in this way they took advantage of the pre-Islamic tendency to believe that whatever happened was the decree of Fate or, in Muslim terms, the will of God.

An important part of the achievement of the Umayyads was that they managed to retain the caliphate within one family for almost a century. This was, of course, in accordance with the Arab practice of selecting the chief of a tribe from a certain family. The achievement, however, shows a good measure of family solidarity and some skill in manipulating Arab institutions. The general method was for the reigning caliph to designate a successor during his lifetime, and to have this successor acclaimed as such by representatives of the main groups of Muslims in a series of councils. Some of the main decisions were doubtless taken by the clan of Umayya in council. We hear of one such meeting in 684 after the young Muʿāwiya II had died leaving no close relatives who were suitable. The whole clan here agreed to support a member of another branch of the family, and thereby retrieved a critical situation. Since the caliphate could be regarded as a federation of tribes, or at least a body of tribes allied to the caliph, it was desirable to obtain the consent of these tribes, and this was done by consulting 'deputations' (*wufūd*) from them. Presumably there were also present in Damascus representatives of the other Meccan clans and of the original Arab inhabitants of Medina (the Anṣār), and these would also be consulted.

One of the chief criticisms levelled against the Umayyads during the ʿAbbāsid period was that they had changed the caliphate into a *mulk*.[9] This is usually translated 'kingdom'. The Arabic word may also mean 'possession', however, and, if so understood, might refer to the Umayyad use of the conception of inheritance and blood-revenge. The basic objection is that Umayyad rule is based on Arab ideas and not on Islamic ways of thinking. The ʿAbbāsids were no less autocratic than the Umayyads, and kept the office of caliph just as much in one family; but they gave fuller outward recognition to the Islamic religion and, at least in their earlier days, to the embryonic class of religious intellectuals. They probably argued that the caliphate remained in their family not as something inherited–they had nothing comparable to the Umayyad plea of blood-revenge–but because on each occasion the person chosen was the best qualified person in view of the charisma (or *baraka*) in the family. Personally the Umayyads were often pious men, despite material luxury and wine-drinking; but their régime depended on pre-Islamic Arab ideas, and these were unsatisfactory for the administration of a large empire.

3. The nature of the caliphate

In the period of a century from the death of Muḥammad the territories occupied and ruled by the Muslims had been extended to the Pyrenees and Morocco in the west and to the Punjab and beyond Samarqand in the east. Despite the size of this empire, however, the office of caliph was still conceived in terms appropriate to the chief of a nomadic tribe; and it is therefore helpful to look once more at conditions in pre-Islamic Arabia.[10]

The chief of a nomadic tribe was usually called a *sayyid* at this period. Each subdivision of the tribe might also have a leader who would be known as a *sayyid*. The *sayyid* at any level had limited powers, and was little more than a *primus inter pares*. Each mature male considered himself as good as the *sayyid*, and would have resented any attempt by the *sayyid* to give him orders. Thus in general the *sayyid* could not command the members of the tribe, but could only persuade. Matters in which there was no established custom were usually decided in the assembly or council of the tribe. Here the personality of the *sayyid*–often an older man–and the skill in oratory which he usually possessed might enable him to obtain the decision he wanted. A younger man would certainly hesitate to oppose a respected *sayyid*, and might not venture even to open his mouth. The *sayyid* had a special responsibility, too, for the external relations of the tribe, and the information he acquired in the course of performing this function might be helpful in the conduct of other business.

The power of the *sayyid* was also limited by powers and functions given to other persons. Leadership in war was usually given by a special decision, and might be for a fixed period only. Mostly, it would seem, it was not the *sayyid* who was appointed as war leader. In some tribes, again, before adopting some new plan the soothsayer (*kāhin*) would be consulted, and this would give some power to the soothsayer at the expense of the *sayyid*. Finally, there were disputes to be settled involving traditional law or custom. If the *sayyid*'s wisdom was respected, disputes between parties within his tribe would be brought to him. In other cases, however, and where he was not sufficiently respected, recourse could be had to those men of wisdom and integrity who were widely accepted as arbiters (sing. *ḥakam*).

Even after the caliph had become ruler of vast territories there was a group of prominent Arabs in Damascus who expected to be consulted on many matters in the same way as the *sayyid* had consulted the notables of the tribe. At many points this made it difficult for the caliph to pursue a steady policy, especially in the last half-century of Umayyad rule when there was bitter feeling between two tribal groups among the Arabs. When one realizes the nature of the institutions with which they worked, one cannot but admire the achievements of the Umayyads. Muʿāwiya in particular was a skilful diplomat and statesman. The caliph, however, had certain advantages over the *sayyid*. An important one was that the caliph was leader in war – a position he had inherited from Muḥammad. For the caliphs leadership in war carried with it the right to make many subordinate appointments connected with the administration of the conquered provinces.

The authority of the caliphs also came to be unquestioned in judicial matters. The old office of arbiter or *ḥakam* died a natural death. The complex new conditions created by the conquests meant that the principles underlying the customary practices of the desert were no longer applicable. In course of time the wisdom of the *ḥakam* was replaced by the 'knowledge' (*ʿilm*) of the scholar in the new 'religious institution' (to be described in Chapter 6). Meanwhile administration had to be carried on and disputes settled. The Constitution of Medina had prescribed that disputes were to be referred to Muḥammad; and in his last years this may be presumed to have been done. The practice continued under the caliphs. The referring of disputes to an arbiter seems to have continued, but with diminishing frequency; or perhaps it would be more correct to say that the natural choice for arbiter came to be the caliph or the provincial governor or the delegate of either. The special office of judge (*qāḍī*) developed during the Umayyad period. At first an administrator might hear disputes as well as perform other duties. There was no fixed body of law to be applied, and each administrator made decisions according to what he thought fit, doubtless following Qur'ānic rules to some extent and also, so far as he was familiar with them, the precedents set by Muḥammad and his own predecessors, especially the latter. In course of time the office of judge became a full-time one, but the basis of decisions remained similar. Gradually, however, there began to appear among the judges some who might be called 'specialists', not in the sense of having received a technical training (since this was not yet in existence) but as having devoted thought to legal matters and having discussed them with like-minded men.[11]

The caliph was also in control of the public treasury. Into this was paid a fifth of the amount of the booty captured on military expeditions, the rents of most of the lands in the conquered provinces, and the poll-tax and other dues from the 'protected groups'. There were some prescriptions in the Qur'ān for the use of this money, but the caliph–and in each province, the governor–had considerable latitude. Some further details about finance will be mentioned in connection with 'the organization of the empire'.

From what has been said it will be seen that the caliph was successor of Muḥammad as head of state. It would not be correct to say that he had succeeded only to the secular aspect of Muḥammad's work, for the caliph might perform certain religious functions, such as leading public worship and delivering the Friday sermon; and after the decline of his temporal power it was held that he validated the legal and social system based on the revealed law. What distinguished the caliphs from Muḥammad was their lack of the office of prophet and their inability to receive further revelations. In later periods it was held that the revelation contained in the Qur'ān was complete and final; and the corollary of this was that no caliph or other ruler had any legislative power. This point may not have been so clearly realized under the Umayyads, however, since there had been little time for theorizing, and they must constantly have been improvising solutions to the problems urgently thrust upon them.

4. The first appearance of Shīʿite ideas

The view of the origin of the caliphate presented above is approximately the Sunnite view. There are also Shīʿite views, however. An extreme one is that Muḥammad designated ʿAlī to succeed him, but that most of Muḥammad's companions refused to recognize ʿAlī. Another view was that ʿAlī, though really designated caliph or imam (leader), and really the best qualified person, allowed Abū-Bakr to take the position. In an Islamic context Shīʿite views naturally led to a rewriting of history, but our present concern is not the precise course of events but the underlying ideas out of which Shīʿism grew.

Apart from the civil war between ʿAlī and Muʿāwiya which broke out in 656, there were a number of incidents in which fighting took place between the Umayyads and the descendants of ʿAlī or their followers. Al-Ḥasan, one of ʿAlī's sons by Muḥammad's daughter Fāṭima, made a half-hearted attempt to claim the caliphate on his father's death, but in the end acquiesced in Muʿāwiya's rule. His full brother al-Ḥusayn made a more determined attempt on the death of Muʿāwiya, but this led to the massacre of al-Ḥusayn and many of 'the family' at Kerbela (680). Before this, in 671, there had been an abortive rising in Kufa of the party of ʿAlī. In 684 a body calling themselves 'the penitents' (because they repented of not giving al-Ḥusayn more support) advanced from Kufa against an Umayyad army on the Syrian border, but were defeated. Shortly afterwards a man called al-Mukhtār held Kufa for about two years in the name of another son of ʿAlī known as Muḥammad ibn-al-Ḥanafiyya ('son of the woman from the tribe of Ḥanīfa', so called to distinguish him from a son, by yet another wife, who was also Muḥammad). After this the Shīʿites (if the name may be given at this period) were quiescent for half a century until the obvious decline of Umayyad power began to suggest to various groups that a revolt might be successful.

The word Shīʿa means 'party', and the complete phrase should be Shīʿat ʿAlī, 'the party of ʿAlī', but this party was sufficiently outstanding to be known simply as 'the party'. The members of 'the party' are said to have sworn to ʿAlī in his lifetime that they would be 'friends of those he befriended, and enemies of those to whom he was hostile'. Whether actually used or not, these words express a distinctive attitude of the Shīʿa. They felt that members of the clan of Hāshim (Muḥammad's clan) had special powers which set them above other men, and they held that the *imām* or 'leader' of the community should be a man with such powers – they usually avoided the term 'caliph'. The idea of the inheriting of special powers within a family was of course truly Arab. At the same time there was a suggestion of anti-democratic feeling in this concept of the imam. He was the person who knew best, so that, if he were obeyed, all would go well, whereas, if the opinion of the common people prevailed, mistakes were likely to be made.

A study of the lists of persons involved in the early risings mentioned above, shows that a significantly large proportion of them came from Arab tribes classed as Yemenite or South-Arabian. This suggests an explanation for the appearance of Shīʿite ideas some twenty-five years after Muḥammad's death. This quarter of a century had been a period of rapid cultural and social change. Men accustomed to the hardships and the freedom of nomadic life in the desert found themselves, when not on campaign in lands far distant from Arabia, spending their time in leisure and material luxury in new camp-cities in Iraq or Egypt or Tunisia. New strains and tensions inevitably arose. Since in a period of stress men tend to revert to a primitive level at which they have experienced security, these men from South Arabia looked round for a superhuman leader–South Arabia had a tradition of many centuries of prosperity under divine kings.[12] (As will be seen in Chapter 5 there was, in response to the same situation, a different type of reversion by men from another background, namely, the Khārijites.) It is to be noted here that, though Shīʿite ideas came to be associated largely with the Persians, their first exponents in the Islamic world were Arabs.

In the period of quiescence from 687 to 737 there appeared the idea of the 'hidden imam'. Muḥammad ibn-al-Ḥanafiyya died (in the usual view) in 700, but some of his followers believed that he was not dead but had gone into concealment, and that he would manifest himself in due course as the Mahdī ('the guided one') who would set all wrongs right and establish justice on earth. The conception of the Mahdī is comparable to the Judaeo-Christian idea of the Messiah, though not always identical. It has, in fact, been used in different ways in Islamic history, and will be mentioned again later.[13] In the Umayyad period the conception of an imam who, after appearing, had gone into concealment had interesting political implications. Belief in such an imam implies that all is not well with the present régime. On the other hand, since the imam is absent, there can be no question of active revolt against the régime for the time being. In other words the régime was accepted *de facto* but not *de jure*.

An important practice which appeared among the Shīʿites during the Umayyad period was that by which a man claimed to be an agent for an imam. Al-Mukhtār had thus claimed to be an agent for Muḥammad ibn-al-Ḥanafiyya, and there were several similar claims under the last Umayyads and yet others under the ʿAbbāsids. It is doubtful whether al-Mukhtār had asked Ibn-al-Ḥanafiyya before claiming to be his agent, but there seems to have been some contact later in which al-Mukhtār gained acceptance. There were other cases where the claim was repudiated. The idea that a man could be an agent of a hidden imam was even more useful–it enabled a gifted politician who was not of 'the family' to put himself forward as leader.

'The family' was still vaguely defined during the Umayyad period. Later the imams were restricted to the descendants of ʿAlī and Fāṭima, but at least until the beginning of the ʿAbbāsid period many persons who could be described as Shīʿites were prepared to acknowledge the charisma of leadership in other branches of the clan of Hāshim. Muḥammad ibn-al-Ḥanafiyya has already been mentioned. Other movements followed imams descended from ʿAlī's brother Jaʿfar and his uncle al-ʿAbbās. The descendants of the latter took advantage of the fact that the qualities needed for an imam were being attributed to the whole clan of Hāshim, and thereby gained the support of many persons of Shīʿite outlook for their revolutionary movement by which they ousted the Umayyad dynasty from the caliphate, and substituted their own, the ʿAbbāsid.

FOUR

THE ORGANIZATION OF EMPIRE

1. The Muslims as a military élite

In most of the expeditions during Muḥammad's lifetime the movable booty was divided among the participants. Certain men who had been unable to participate because Muḥammad had given them other duties were counted as participants. In the case of the larger expeditions the division of the booty was carried out in the efficient way one might have expected from merchants skilled in large commercial undertakings. Most of the actual handling of the goods – whether camels, cattle, sheep, slaves or material objects – was done by dealers, and each man probably got his share in money or in goods bought from the dealers. A fifth of the proceeds was paid to Muḥammad for the public treasury. A new principle came into play, however, with the expedition against Khaybar in 628. The Jewish farmers there were not expelled but allowed to go on cultivating on condition that they paid a proportion of their produce, primarily dates, to the Muslims. A similar principle was followed under Abū-Bakr and ʿUmar, and as lands were conquered the inhabitants were assigned certain amounts as land-tax (*kharāj*) in addition to a poll-tax (*jizya*) of so much per head. The precise terms varied according to whether a community submitted when first summoned to do so, or surrendered only after being defeated in fighting. Even in the latter case, however, the terms were not unduly onerous.

A major military and financial reform is attributed to the caliph ʿUmar about the year 640, and is commonly referred to as the Dīwān of ʿUmar. A Dīwān is here a 'register', and this was a register of all the men in the armies, arranged according to their tribes. At the same time, however, the Dīwān fixed the stipends they were to receive out of the taxes from the conquered lands. The stipends were graded on the principle that those who had become Muslims at an earlier date should receive more. There are several variants of the list of categories, probably indicating that the amounts and categories changed from time to time. One list runs as follows[1]:

those who fought at Badr	(dirhams) 5000
those who were Muslims before al-Ḥudaybiya (628)	4000
Muslims by the reign of Abū-Bakr (634)	3000
fighters at Qādisiyya and in Syria	2000
Muslims after Qādisiyya and the Yarmūk	1000
various minor groups	500, 300, 250, 200
Muḥammad's widows	10,000
wives of men of Badr	500
wives of next three classes	400, 300, 200
wives of others, and children	100

One of the results of the principle on which the Dīwān was constructed was the creation of a new élite or nobility or upper class, replacing the former Arab nobility, whose position seems to have depended only partly on descent but even more on their current wealth and prosperity. The conflict of interests between the old and the new nobilities affects the politics of the Umayyad period. The Umayyads belonged to the old upper class, whereas ʿAlī and most of the clan of Hāshim had risen through their support of the new religion. Some of the supporters of ʿAlī were not men with Shīʿite ideas but, like the Anṣār or Muslims of Medina, men who had benefited from the principle of 'priority in Islam'.[2]

The reorganization associated with the Dīwān of ʿUmar made possible the vast conquests. Had the Arabs settled on the conquered lands or even become absentee landlords in the neighbouring towns, there would have been no army to press on into fresh regions. The system of stipends, however, made it feasible for the Arabs to spend a large portion of their time in campaigning. At first the armies were almost exclusively Arab. Non-Arabs who became Muslims were at length admitted to the army, but at first almost grudgingly and without equal rights to a share of the spoils. Even with the system of stipends Arab man-power was stretched to its utmost, and the later conquests of the Umayyads were only possible through the accession of man-power from the Berbers in the west and the Persians, especially the Khorasanians, in the east.

The whole system of the Dīwān of ʿUmar eventually broke down and disappeared, but the stages are not clearly indicated by historians. After tasting luxury men were unwilling to undergo the hardships and dangers of distant campaigns. This happened even in Muḥammad's lifetime. After the first wave of expansion which took the Muslims beyond the frontiers of Iraq in the east and of Egypt in the west, it was impracticable for the Arabs, even if they wanted to do so, to return to Arabia between expeditions. Camp cities developed and men found occupations to engage their energies and add to their income during the period they spent in these cities. Special inducements became necessary to persuade them to go on campaign. Especially after many of the previous inhabitants of Iraq had become Muslims it was not necessary that all Muslims should fight, and indeed not all had the requisite qualities. Thus soldiering became a specialized calling, and some of the troops might be called semi-professionals. The earlier ʿAbbāsid caliphs relied to a considerable extent on their Khorasanian troops. About 835, however, the caliph al-Muʿtaṣim formed a bodyguard most of whom, including the officers, were Turkish mercenaries. Such a change must have meant the end of the enlisting of ordinary Muslims. Stipends are still mentioned occasionally until about 850; but presumably they were given only to those who actually took part in campaigns, and they may have been a relatively small part of their income.

Even after most of the fighting came to be done by professionals, these had always to be Muslims. In times of special emergency other Muslims might be asked to volunteer for military service. There was no question of any non-Muslim, a member of the 'protected minorities' (to be described presently), taking part in the military expeditions of an Islamic state.[3] This tradition has never been abandoned, at least not until very recent times. In the Ottoman empire military service continued to be only for Muslims. In the middle of the nineteenth century the 'protected minorities' were filled with dismay when it was suggested that they should share a common Ottoman nationality with the Muslims, since this would have meant liability for military service. Perhaps this reluctance to allow non-Muslims to fight was linked with the fact that most of the wars in which an Islamic army would fight would be 'holy wars', fought 'in the way of God'. Sir John Bagot Glubb (Glubb Pasha), speaking from long experience of military affairs in the Arab world, finds that there reappears in recent Arab revolutions 'the old idea that the army is the guardian of the nation's morals'.[4] Thus is the contemporary Islamic world linked with its roots in the past.

2. The 'protected minorities'

The relation of the Muslims to the Jews and the Christians had been a problem from the time of the Hijra. The Qur'ān speaks of the revelation to Muḥammad as repeating and confirming previous revelations, especially the Torah of the Jews (or Old Testament) and the Injīl ('evangel') or New Testament of the Christians. Muḥammad consequently expected Jews and Christians to accept him as the Messenger of God. It soon became clear that the Jews of Medina were not prepared to do this. As for the Christians, there were so few contacts during Muḥammad's early years at Medina that he may still have hoped they would accept him. The Jews of Medina apparently had a treaty relationship with Muḥammad from the beginning. When it came to hostilities with Jews outside Medina – those at Khaybar – they were accepted, on their defeat and surrender, into the Pax Islamica, but as a payment for this protection they had to pay to the Muslims a proportion of their date harvest. There are also reports of treaties with the Christians of Ayla (biblical Elath, modern Akaba), the Jews of Maqnā near by, and other small groups encountered during the expedition to Tabūk in 630. In general these small groups were said to receive 'the protection (*jiwār*, *dhimma*) of God and of his Messenger'; they retained their internal structure of government; and in return they made a payment, usually in kind.[5]

This system is a development of the Arab practice whereby a strong tribe 'protected' weaker tribes and groups. It was a matter of honour for the strong tribe to demonstrate to all that its protection was effective. This was indeed a measure of its strength. The early Muslim rulers had a similar attitude. On one occasion 'Umar is reported to have repaid money to the people of Damascus when he had to evacuate the town and therefore could not continue to protect them. It has been suggested that the Islamic system of 'protected minorities' in its developed form was based on Byzantine and Sasanian practices. While it is possible that these may have affected minor details, the general principle is sufficiently close to nomadic Arab practice for this to be taken as the origin of the system.

During the conquests the general principle was widely applied but with no uniformity. The precise arrangements entered into with any group depended on the previous structure of government and the attitude of the group's members to the Muslims. With regard to attitude the later Muslim theorists distinguished between groups which submitted voluntarily without fighting and those which were forced to submit by military defeat; they are said to have submitted either *ṣulḥan* or *ʿanwatan*. The treatment of the latter was usually less favourable than that of the former, but not necessarily harsh. All Jewish, Christian and other non-Muslim groups within the Islamic empire had an arrangement of the kind described. The three elements found in Muḥammad's time are always found, namely, protection from external enemies, internal autonomy, and a payment to the treasury. In the case of the payments a distinction was later made between land-tax (*kharāj*) and poll-tax (*jizya*); but the names and the precise nature of the taxes varied much to begin with. These 'protected minorities' were known collectively as *ahl adh-dhimma*, 'people of the security-undertaking', and a member of such a group was a *dhimmī*.[6] In the Ottoman empire the term 'millet' (Arabic *milla*) was commonly used for the group.

While this system was primarily a political one, it was always assumed that such a minority-group or millet was homogeneous in respect of religion. This was part of the Qur'ānic intellectual outlook, implicit in the idea (already noted) that a messenger was sent by God to a tribe or community. The religious communities familiar to the Muslims were primarily the Jews and the Christians, but it was assumed that there were many others, since there had been many messengers. The privilege of becoming a 'protected minority' was only given to communities which followed a messenger or prophet. Pagans in Arabia, as explained above, had no choice but 'Islam or the sword'; that is to say, if a group was not prepared to accept

Islam, it had either to fight the Muslims or leave the regions controlled by them. The various 'protected minorities' were, as followers of prophets, known as *ahl al-kitāb*, 'the people of the Book' or 'scripturaries'. A very liberal interpretation, however, was given to the conception of a monotheistic religion with written scriptures; and Zoroastrians and, later, Hindus and Buddhists became 'protected minorities'.

The millet system had numerous advantages and worked well for many centuries, and indeed until the collapse of the Ottoman empire. Though it has now broken down in the Middle East, vestiges of it remain, e.g. in the form of separate courts for various religious communities. The problem of minorities in the contemporary Middle East is a legacy from the millet system,[7] and an indication of the failure so far to find any adequate replacement for it. In the early days of the Islamic empire the Christian inhabitants of Egypt and the Fertile Crescent were probably better off as *dhimmīs* under Muslim Arab rulers than they had been under Byzantine Greeks. One of the reasons why the system worked well was that among the pre-Islamic Arabs it had been a matter of honour for the desert tribe to show that its protection was effective, and something of this attitude to the *dhimmīs* passed to Muslim rulers. On the whole there was more genuine toleration of non-Muslims under Islam than there was of non-Christians in medieval Christian states. There were exceptions, of course. When times were hard and difficult, non-Muslims would tend to get the worst of it. Occasionally, too, a ruler, in order to divert animosity from himself, would encourage the mob to vent its feelings on the *dhimmīs*. On the whole, however, the 'protected minorities' had a tolerable existence.

There was one serious disadvantage for the *dhimmī*, however: he was always, as it were, a second-class citizen. Through the centuries this one factor exercised a constant pressure on the *dhimmī* to become a Muslim. There was a steady trickle of converts, and with the passage of time this completely altered the proportion of Muslims to non-Muslims. Immediately after the Arab conquests the *dhimmīs* constituted the vast majority of the inhabitants of the new provinces, but in course of time, because of the conversions and other adverse factors, their numbers dwindled and the Muslims formed the vast majority.

In North Africa and Central Asia the Christians disappeared altogether. Small Jewish communities managed to survive in several Islamic lands, but some of these have moved out during the present century. The Ottoman conquests in Europe in the sixteenth and seventeenth centuries again brought large numbers of Christians under Muslim rule; but the decline of the Ottoman empire and the support they received from Western Europe and Russia enabled most of them to regain independence.

3. Provincial administration

In an earlier section of this chapter the Muslims were spoken of as a military élite in the Islamic empire during the Umayyad period. This was perhaps a euphemism for 'occupying army'. That was in fact how the imperial administration began, and it was only gradually, as conversions to Islam increased, that the Muslim élite–the first-class citizens–came to include many who took no part in soldiering. When provinces were first conquered, however, administration through the army was the normal practice. The inhabitants of the province were given the status of 'protected minorities' and retained most of their internal administration, in so far as the actual men involved were still available and had not fled. This administration, however, was now responsible to the general of the Muslim army and handed over to him or to his financial officer the appropriate taxes. Thus the general was directly responsible for administering only the Muslims. At first these consisted solely of the men in the army, but when camp-cities were established in the provinces, and when Muslims settled in existing cities like Damascus, there were Muslim civilians also. Nevertheless the basic simplicity of the system contributed to the rapidity with which the Arabs established an empire.

The general in command of a province, or governor, was at first called *ʿāmil*, 'agent', or less frequently *amīr*, 'commander'.[8] To begin with, too, he mostly selected his own subordinates. In course of time the word *ʿāmil*, 'agent', came to be applied exclusively to the man in charge of the finances of the administration, including the collection of the taxes; and under the later Umayyads he was usually appointed by the caliph directly and might be almost as powerful as the governor. Another of the duties of the governor when he came to have Muslim civilians under him was to adjudicate in disputes. In course of time, however, this duty was entrusted to a *qāḍī* or 'judge' who became more and more of a specialist.

In the course of the centuries and with the rise and fall of many dynasties there were naturally changes in the details of provincial administration. No novel principles, however, of sufficient importance to be mentioned in this study appear to have emerged.

FIVE

MEMBERSHIP OF THE COMMUNITY

1. The Khārijite movement

Like much else in Islamic history the Khārijite movement has both a political and a religious aspect. It may be regarded either as a series of political revolts or as a series of theological heresies. The Arabic word rendered as 'Khārijites' is *Khawārij*, which is the plural of the participle *khārij*, 'one going out or seceding', though a single Khārijite is a *Khārijī*. The movement is held to have begun a year or two after the accession of ʿAlī when a group of his supporters, allegedly disapproving of his attitude to the Arbitration, 'went out' or 'seceded' from his army. Some of the first seceders ʿAlī was able to reconcile, but there was a second secession which ended in the massacre of most of the participants. After this five further Khārijite revolts are recorded during the reign of ʿAlī, each involving about 200 men, and some sixteen revolts during the reign of Muʿāwiya with from 30 to 500 participants.[1] The revolts against ʿAlī show that the Khārijite movement was not specifically anti-Umayyad.

The theoretical basis of the Khārijite movement was a Qur'ānic slogan, *lā ḥukm illā li-llāh*, meaning 'no decision but God's' or 'the decision is God's alone'.[2] This was further interpreted to imply that political decisions must be based on the word of God, the Qur'ān; and the Khārijite objection to the Arbitration was presumably that it was not in fact so based—perhaps the arbiters recognized the validity of the Umayyad claim to have inherited the caliphate from ʿUthmān along with the duty of revenge. The first Khārijites also held that they were following the murderers of ʿUthmān, who justified the murder on the ground that ʿUthmān had broken God's law by not inflicting a penalty prescribed in the Qur'ān; it is to be noted, however, that virtually none of those involved in the murder are to be found among the Khārijites.

Closely connected with this slogan was the doctrine–both theological and political–that the person who had committed a grave sin was thereby excluded from the community. To the modern occidental reader this may not sound a very serious matter, but to the Arab it was of the utmost importance. It has to be remembered that according to the outlook of the desert a human being as such has no rights. The security of life and goods is linked with membership of a community capable of protecting him. If a man's conduct was felt to be outrageous, his tribe might expel him; his life would then be in danger until he found someone else to protect him. At one point Muḥammad's clan withdrew protection from him, presumably because he was alleged to have slandered the ancestors of the clan; and he was unable to return to Mecca after a journey in the neighbourhood until he had found another clan willing to protect him.[3] When the protecting body was not just a clan or tribe but the whole community of Muslims, exclusion was much more serious since one had to go far afield to find alternative protectors. The full justification for the murder of ʿUthmān was that by breaking a Qur'ānic prescription he was excluded from the community and his blood made 'lawful' for any Muslim–that is, to kill him would be no sin. Further, since he was now unlawfully usurping the position of head of the community of Muslims, it was even a duty to kill him.

The doctrine that grave sin excludes from the community thus had serious political implications, especially when any small group could decide on the particular application. The doctrine was in fact pushed to extremes by an insurrectionary group known as the Azraqites (or Azāriqa).[4] They were little better than brigands, and for more than a dozen years from 684 (during the troubled period of the war between the Umayyads and Ibn-az-Zubayr) they terrorized Basra and the region to the east of it in Persia. Their distinctive principle was that not to join their insurrection–not to make the *hijra* to their camp, as they put it–was itself a grave sin. Thus only the relatively small body of Azraqite terrorists were Muslims; all the other persons usually called Muslims were, in Azraqite eyes, unbelievers. This meant, too, that all these 'unbelievers' could be killed without sin; and the Azraqites in fact proceeded to massacre them on a large scale as opportunity offered. Even after the Umayyads had crushed Ibn-az-Zubayr, it took them a year or two to suppress the remnants of the Azraqites.

Not all the men of Khārijite sympathies in Basra were prepared to go out to the camp of the Azraqites and to approve of their indiscriminate killing of all opponents. Those who remained, however, had to find some way of squaring their doctrines with their practice. In particular they had to justify their readiness to go on living under the governorship of one who in their eyes was not a Muslim. A subordinate point was whether they were prepared to allow 'believing' women to marry men whom they regarded as 'unbelievers'. Many subtle points were made in the course of the discussions. The most important were those connected with the definition of 'unbeliever' (*kāfir*) and 'polytheist' (*mushrik*). Some argued that these terms could not be applied to a man unless he was ignorant of God or denied him. Some were prepared to admit that the ordinary non-Khārijite, though not a Muslim, was at least a 'monotheist' (*muwaḥḥid*). In this way they began to admit that membership of the community involved something more than avoidance of sins, namely, an element of intellectual belief. The most important sect among the moderate Khārijites are the Ibāḍites, of whom small pockets still exist in Algeria, Oman and elsewhere.[5]

From a general historical standpoint the events involving the Khārijites are unimportant. Yet the ideas implicit in the movement have contributed more to Islamic politics than appears at first sight. Briefly, the point about to be made is that the Khārijite and Shīʿite movements are opposite responses to the same situation—that produced by the transformation of Arab nomads into the military élite of an empire. When they felt insecure the Shīʿites turned for safety to a charismatic leader because of their roots in the South Arabian idea of divine kingship. Similarly, the Khārijites in their insecurity turned for safety to the charismatic community, as it may be called. Many of the Khārijite leaders came from certain North Arabian tribes, which had had no experience of divine kingship, but in which presumably the tribe and the tribal stock had been highly regarded.[6]

In support of the view that the Khārijites in their quest for security looked to the charismatic community, one may point to the way in which they formed small groups not unlike nomadic sub-tribes or clans–as if they were trying to restore the former groups in which they had lived, but on an Islamic basis. The resemblance of the Khārijite bands to nomadic groups is increased by their excellence in poetry and oratory, matters for which some of the old desert tribes had been famed. The chief evidence, however, for the influence of the idea of the charismatic community on their activity is their exclusion of the grave sinner from the group. This is to be linked with the fact that they spoke of their group as 'the people of Paradise' and everyone else as 'the people of Hell'. Since a grave sinner, they held, went to Hell, to retain in the group someone bound for Hell was to endanger the whole group–it would no longer be 'the people of Paradise', and the individual associated with it would no longer be assured of Paradise. In contemporary terms one could say that the essential belief here was that through membership of this community the individual life attained significance.

On the political plane the Khārijites criticized the following of a leader on the ground that, if the leader erred, all would go astray. On the other hand it does not appear that they held any view comparable to that of *vox populi vox Dei*. There is indeed a saying ascribed to Muḥammad (but probably a later invention) to the effect that 'my community will not agree on an error'; and the agreement or consensus of the community later became one of the roots of law. For the Khārijites, however, the underlying idea was probably a development of pre-Islamic conceptions of nobility and the lack of it. The Islamic community was a 'noble' one, since it was divinely constituted and had a divine rule of life; and so it is bound to act well. That is to say, the charismatic community avoids mistakes and attains security in so far as it follows its divinely given rules.

2. The wider community of true believers

The Khārijites overemphasized something of great importance for Islam–the idea that the Islamic community is a charismatic one, that is, divinely founded and ensuring a superior type of life for its members. Gradually, as they continued to live among non-Khārijite Muslims, the moderate Khārijites realized that they could not maintain their basic principle that they alone would go to Paradise and that all the non-Khārijite Muslims would go to Hell. Some of the moderates began to 'suspend judgement' on certain questions, such as the lawfulness of selling 'believing' slave-girls to be concubines of 'unbelievers'. Eventually the main Khārijite thesis that 'grave sin excludes from the community' was explicitly challenged by a party known as the Murji'ites. Their contrary thesis was that the question whether a particular sinner belonged to 'the people of Hell' and was excluded from the community must be postponed to God's decision on the Last Day; it cannot be answered by man. The principle that the grave sinner is not excluded from the community was accepted by nearly all Muslims, and this part of Murji'ite views is thus accepted by the main body of Muslims. In the books on theological sects various groups of Murji'ites are described and regarded as heretical; but this is in respect of some secondary matters and not in respect of their main thesis.

The principle that, despite grave sin, a man remained a member of the community had various practical effects. When all 'grave sins' are punished by exclusion from the community (and possibly death), there is a tendency to reduce the number of acts regarded as 'grave sin'. Good government, however, requires the punishment of crime, even when that is not sufficiently serious to warrant expulsion or death. The Murji'ite principle thus justified the punishment of criminals without excluding them from the community. It also justified the behaviour of Muslims who continued to live under a ruler of whom they disapproved and who were not constantly looking for opportunities to kill him. The Murji'ites could thus criticize the Umayyads and yet at the same time support them. In this they exemplified a prominent tendency among Muslims, namely, to avoid any rebellion against a *de facto* ruler.

The result of the general acceptance of the central Murji'ite principle was that the idea of the charismatic community was applied to the whole body of Muslims. The Muslims, as a whole, were 'the people of Paradise'. Crime had indeed to be punished; but the theologians held out hope that the Muslim criminal might in the end enter Paradise. The doctrine that found widest acceptance was that all Muslims who committed sins would be punished for them; the punishment might be in this life, or it might be in Hell in the future life; if the latter were the case, however, they would only be in Hell for a limited period and would then by Muḥammad's intercession be admitted to Paradise. The Islamic community is thus in a real sense the community through which a man attains salvation or the supreme goal in life. One is reminded of the Christian assertion *extra ecclesia nulla salus*.

So far the idea of the charismatic community has been presented in the religious terminology in which it normally appears in Islam. Yet it is a matter of concern to the politician, Islamic or occidental, irrespective of his personal attitude to religion. The great body of Sunnite Muslims, because of their beliefs about the community, have a deep devotion to it. It is the community which has given their lives significance, has given them an identity of which they are proud. Many of the achievements of Islamic culture–such as the elaboration of a vast system of law and morals–have been possible through the energies released by zeal for the community. One of the factors leading to the spread of Islam in tropical Africa and south-east Asia is the self-confidence of the ordinary Muslim, arising from his pride in his community. In short, even at the present day the attitudes of Muslims to the Islamic community can be disregarded by a statesman only at his peril.

3. The conditions of membership of the community

The early Islamic community was, in occidental terms, both religious and political. Membership therefore tended to be defined in religious terms, and this leads to the curious situation that membership of a political community is defined in religious terms. Thus, even from the standpoint of a study of political ideas, it is useful to look briefly at the religious definitions of membership.

The term most frequently applied in the Qur'ān to Muḥammad's followers is 'the believers' (*mu'minūn*). Much less frequent is the term which after his death became the standard one, *muslimūn* or 'Muslims', meaning 'those who submit, *sc.* to God'. Both words are participles used as nouns. To them there correspond the verbal nouns *īmān*, 'faith', and *islām*, 'submission'. Unfortunately the English word 'faith' and its European equivalents have connotations that are not appropriate to the Arabic *īmān*, which in some contexts means no more than 'what makes a man a believer'. In early times Islam appears to have been also called 'the Ḥanīfite religion' and the individual Muslim a *ḥanīf*, 'usually taken to mean a pure monotheist who is neither Jew nor Christian'; but this usage was abandoned, and need not concern us further here.[7] (It may be remarked in passing that, since the word 'Muslim' properly means a person, 'one submitting', and is not a general adjective, it is best not applied to abstract things like art and culture. The appropriate adjective is 'Islamic'. Thus 'Muslim' is not like 'Christian' which is both noun and adjective but rather like 'Celt' and 'Jew' which are only nouns. Although one can use a noun as an adjective in English, this is not done where there is an adjective available; it would be strange to talk of 'Celt art' or 'Jew religion'.)

In Muḥammad's lifetime there were two different criteria of what made a man a believer or a Muslim. The first criterion referred to practice and was chiefly applied to groups and not to individuals. It was the performance of the public worship (*ṣalāt*) and the payment of the 'legal alms' (*zakāt*–a kind of tithe, but sometimes constituting a form of tribute). This twofold criterion is frequently mentioned in the Qur'ān. The second criterion was rather an act of allegiance to the community and was more personal. It consisted in the repetition of the confession of faith or 'witnessing' (*shahāda*), that is, the formula, 'I bear witness there is no god but God, Muḥammad is the Messenger of God'. The story is told of a certain pagan Arab, whose name was on the list of a dozen or so persons proscribed at the conquest of Mecca, that he escaped death by remaining in hiding for a time, then suddenly appearing before Muḥammad and repeating the formula before he could be arrested; the implication of the story is that the mere repetition made him a Muslim and cancelled his misdeeds as a pagan. The first half of the formula is based on a number of verses of the Qur'ān, but the whole formula may not have been used as a formula till long after Muḥammad's death, since the story was probably elaborated in the course of transmission. Nevertheless something of the nature of this criterion was doubtless used in Muḥammad's lifetime.

In addition to these two criteria, a prerequisite of membership of the community until the end of the Umayyad period was that a man should be an Arab; consequently non-Arabs, on becoming Muslims, had also to become 'clients' (*mawālī*) of Arab tribes. This was presumably because the Islamic community was regarded as a body of Arab tribes in alliance with Muḥammad or the caliph. This point need not concern us further, however.

The Khārijite movement develops the first criterion in that it is concerned with practice. It was an attempt to make a minimum standard of behaviour a condition of continuing membership. The attempt was unsuccessful, and instead nearly the whole community accepted the view that failures in practice, whether crimes or the omission of worship, did not exclude a man from the community. This meant that in subsequent discussions the second criterion, the confession of faith, was prominent. Most scholars agreed that there must be both belief in the heart (that is, mind) and confession with the lips, but they disagreed about the necessity of practice. Some held that a man with a high standard of practice of his religion had more 'faith' than one with a lower standard. Some objected to this that 'faith' could not increase or decrease, since it was indivisible–presumably they understood 'faith' as that which makes a man a member of the community; clearly a man must either be a member of the community or not a member; there is no half-way house.

Creeds, or statements of theological doctrines to be accepted, were drawn up by many individual Muslims. These were usually accepted by their immediate followers. Some found much wider acceptance, but none ever came to hold a position comparable to that of the Nicene Creed, for example, in Christendom. This is partly because there was no body capable of making a creed authoritative for all Muslims. It followed that there were divergences of view about the points of doctrine a man must believe if he was to be considered a Muslim. Some later theologians wanted the acceptance of an elaborate creed made obligatory for all Muslims. A few even wanted the ordinary Muslim to be able to give a rational proof of each article of faith. None of this was generally accepted, however. The one point on which the great majority of Muslims agreed was that *shirk* or 'idolatry' (literally 'associating, *sc.* other beings with God') entailed ceasing to be a Muslim. This was, in effect, an insistence on the first half of the *shahāda*, namely, 'there is no god but God'. In a sense the second half had also to be accepted, namely 'Muḥammad is the Messenger of God'; for to leave Islam for any other community, even the Jewish or Christian, was apostasy (*ridda*) and was punishable by death.

The opposite of *īmān*, 'faith', is usually taken to be *kufr*, 'unbelief'; and correspondingly the 'unbeliever' or 'infidel' is a *kāfir* (plural *kāfirūn* or *kuffār*). Originally the infidel was someone outside the Islamic community; for the extreme Khārijites the grave sinner became an infidel. When theological discussions became frequent, however, it became common for a theologian to say that some opponent's view of which he strongly disapproved amounted to *kufr*, 'unbelief'. They even coined a word *takfīr* to mean 'the declaration that (someone) is an unbeliever'. Since there was never wide agreement that a particular doctrine was *kufr*, the 'declaration of unbelief' came to be without practical effect. Al-Ghazālī (d. 1111) wrote a book criticizing the indiscriminate use of the *takfīr* or 'declaration of unbelief'. In the case of al-Ḥallāj the mystic, condemned to death for heresy in 922, Louis Massignon, who studied his life and teaching exhaustively, showed that, before he could be condemned, he had to be accused not merely of *kufr* or 'unbelief' but of *zandaqa*; this, though almost synonymous with *kufr*, had the further connotation that it concerned a heretical belief menacing the security of the state.[8] The trial of al-Ḥallāj illustrates the tendency of Muslim scholars, even when verbally very fierce, to avoid punishing other Muslims for merely religious crimes.

From the standpoint of an interest in political ideas this theological development gives insight into the nature of the solidarity of the Islamic community. It is first and foremost a natural community, a community into which one is born. Though Islam is often described as a missionary religion, Muslims have seldom boasted about converts to Islam, and indeed have tended to hide the fact of conversions. Presumably they felt that, while converts were greatly benefiting themselves, the religion of Islam was not made any more certain or more glorious by the adherence of these men to it. The character of Islam as a natural community is further shown by the reluctance of Muslims to expel anyone from the community for deviance in belief or liturgical practice. It is chiefly idolatry or definite attachment to a rival religious community that leads to such expulsion; it is felt that the man guilty of one of these has gone beyond what his brother Muslims can accept. On the positive side the *shahāda* or confession of faith is, politically, the expression of a general acceptance of the values of Islam and its world-view or intellectual outlook. As one looks at Islam over the centuries one is impressed by the degree to which communal solidarity has been maintained. One of the factors contributing to this end has been the creation of a homogeneous intellectual outlook, which has partly incorporated and partly supplanted previous intellectual outlooks in the territories where Islam is now dominant (a matter to be studied further in the next chapter). The topics dealt with in the present chapter are important as showing some of the underlying structures of this solidarity.

SIX

THE RELIGIOUS INSTITUTION

1. The formation of the religious institution

It has often been observed that the political development of the Islamic world differs completely from that of Europe because of the absence of a Church. The obvious truth of this remark, however, conceals the fact that there is in Islam an institution, or perhaps one should say a series of institutions, through which many of the political functions of the Church are performed.[1] Thus one of the points of interest in a study such as the present is the contrast between the working of the religious institutions in the two cultures. It is therefore desirable to attempt to give an account of the growth and nature of the religious institution, as it has been called, in the Islamic world.

During the lifetime of Muḥammad there was probably little that could be called religious study or discussion. Many Muslims, of course, memorized large parts of the Qur'ān; a few wrote it down. The more responsible men perhaps discussed the application of the Qur'ānic rules. The Traditions suggest, however, that if Muslims were in doubt about any point, they went and asked Muḥammad. The first serious discussions of religious questions took place in the course of the civil war which followed the murder of ʿUthmān in 656. Like all the early discussions among Muslims these had both a religious and a political aspect. It was indeed impossible for Muslim Arabs at this period to discuss anything except in religious terms, since the system of ideas found in the Qur'ān had come to dominate their whole thought world. Even the opponents of the Islamic state, who revolted against the government in Medina on Muḥammad's death – the 'wars of the apostasy' – had to give their revolts a religious basis by claiming to be prophets on an equal footing with Muḥammad. It was therefore not surprising that the political and social discontent which found an outlet in the Khārijite movement expressed itself in religious terms.

Until at least the year 900 or 950, and perhaps for longer, all religious discussions among Muslims had political or social relevance. For the moment, however, the religious aspect may be looked at by itself. The discussions stimulated by the Khārijites continued and grew in volume. It became a feature of life in the Islamic cities that men sat about in the mosques and discussed all sorts of questions. In such discussions those with the qualities needed for intellectual leadership stood out above their fellows. A man of this type would come to be acknowledged as informal president of such a group. Then he would make a habit of sitting in a certain place, and the circle would form round him. The next stage was that he began to give teaching to those who sat in his circles. It is difficult to give exact dates for the stages of a gradual process like this, but it would seem that by about the year 700 something not far removed from formal teaching was being given in the chief cities. Certainly by the year 750 there were groups of men with a common mind on questions of religious law and other matters. From one standpoint these can be called 'the ancient schools of law'. From another standpoint a historian like Julius Wellhausen could speak of them as the 'pious opposition' to the Umayyads. There were many different strands of thought, however, among these people, and one man held views on most subjects. In respect of the Umayyad period, however, it is better to speak of 'the general religious movement'.[2]

Most of those who were interested in legal matters in fact supported the 'Abbāsids, since the Umayyads often followed pre-Islamic Arab custom rather than specifically Islamic rules. In consequence of this support the 'ancient schools' in particular received a measure of recognition from the 'Abbāsid government. Many of the judges were now chosen from men whose legal scholarship was approved by the 'schools'. Eventually this came to be the case with all judges and holders of positions in which legal knowledge was required. In return, however, for recognition the 'Abbāsids brought pressure to bear on the legal schools in the main cities in order to secure a measure of uniformity. In this aim the 'Abbāsids were partly successful, and there came to be a wide area of agreement; but all variations were not smoothed away, and there are still among Sunnite Muslims four different legal schools or 'rites' – the Mālikite, Ḥanafite, Shāfiʿite, and Ḥanbalite.

Many difficulties had to be overcome before the jurists could produce a complete system of law for an empire. The Qur'ān contained a number of legal rules, but these were chiefly concerned with matters on which decisions were urgently required by the nascent community at Medina. In other matters Muḥammad and his subordinates had followed pre-Islamic custom. At first the 'ancient schools' of law were answering the question 'What ought to be done?', and would simply declare 'our view is so-and-so'. One result of the pressure for uniformity by the ʿAbbāsid government was to force the jurists to give reasons for holding that 'so-and-so ought to be done'. In the end the criterion accepted by all Sunnite jurists was that, where there was no explicit Qur'ānic rule, the decision should be based on a Tradition from the Prophet. The word 'Tradition' (Arabic *ḥadīth*) is here used in a technical sense (which I indicate by a capital) to mean an anecdote about something Muḥammad said or did. It was further agreed by Muslim scholars that in a 'sound' or authentic Tradition the anecdote should be accompanied by a chain of transmitters, somewhat as follows: 'A said that he once heard B recounting how he had heard C saying that he had been present when D told how Muḥammad had said ...' A, B, C and D were real persons, and in course of time biographical dictionaries were compiled from which one could verify the possibility of contacts between A and B, B and C, and C and D. D had to be someone who had known Muḥammad personally, and such persons are technically known as 'Companions'. The general acceptance of this conception of Tradition is ascribed to ash-Shāfiʿī (d. 820), the founder of the Shāfiʿite school of jurisprudence.

The jurists had not only to deal with the difficulties of their subject-matter. There was also a class of persons associated with the ʿAbbāsid administration who were hostile to the jurists. This was the group known as 'secretaries'. They were what we should call civil servants or administrators. Many of them were descendants of men who had held similar positions under the Sasanian empire, and they appear to have received their training by a kind of apprenticeship 'on the job'. The 'secretaries' were one element in the 'autocratic bloc' which for the first century of ʿAbbāsid rule (750-850) was engaged in a fierce struggle for power with the 'constitutionalist bloc' – this struggle will be described more fully in the next chapter. The 'secretaries' wanted an 'autocratic' caliph, since they actually wielded much of the caliph's power; and they resented the jurists as upstarts who were limiting the caliph's power by extending to the whole of life the divine law to which the caliph must submit, and of which the jurists were the authoritative exponents. By the year 850 it had become clear to the ʿAbbāsid rulers that their empire was most likely to be stable if they looked for support to the elements of the 'constitutionalist bloc' and accepted in the main their conception of government.

Since the adoption of a new policy by the government just before 850 meant that the Sunnite form of Islam was dominant throughout the lands of the ʿAbbāsid caliphate, the religious institution may be said to have established itself. The work of systematization continued for at least another century, but the main lines of development had been decided by 850. The life of the Islamic community in all its aspects was to be based on the Sharīʿa or divinely revealed law. This at any rate was the theory, though, as we shall see, there were exceptions. The religious institution consisted of the recognized exponents of the Sharīʿa and the intellectual structure associated with it; these are the ulema (*ʿulamā'*, literally 'knowers'). The ulema had control of the higher education which was taking shape. There were various specializations among them, but for reasons which should now be obvious, the core of Islamic higher education was jurisprudence. It will be useful at this point to look more closely at the content of this higher education and its place in the life of the community.

2. The formation of the Islamic world-view

The Islamic religious institution as just described may have given the impression of being a body which was loosely organized and had little real power. Yet among the achievements of this institution was the production of a world-view or Weltanschauung or ideational system which dominated the thinking of the millions of inhabitants of the heartlands of Islam, and was a strong influence on the thinking of all other Muslims. This was not simply a case of filling a vacuum. When Islam came on the scene, the lands which are now its heartlands were part of the heartlands of Christendom and the seat of flourishing Christian intellectual systems. For the most part these Hellenistic Christian systems disappeared and were replaced by the Islamic world-view. This result probably did not follow from any deliberate policy on the part of the Muslim intellectual leaders, but came about through the operation of certain factors in the make-up of the first Muslim Arabs. It is therefore important to try to understand these factors and the manner in which their operation led to the totalitarian dominance of the Islamic world-view.

The world-view of the pre-Islamic Arabs was primitive. History for them was no more than the rise and decline of tribes. They had no sense of a linear development in history. Perhaps because of this they were not interested in the distant past or the origins of the cosmos. The events of their lives they held to be controlled by an impersonal force they called 'Time' or 'the days', with some connotation of 'Fate'. All in all this world-view was so jejune that one might speak of a vacuum. For those who became Muslims this vacuum was filled by the system of ideas expressed or implied in the Qur'ān. Except when they were considering pre-Islamic topics, it was impossible for Muslim Arabs to *think* in any other than Qur'ānic terms. Even the Arabs who remained for a time on the fringe of the Islamic state were influenced in their thinking by the Qur'ānic ideas. Since the political thinking of pre-Islamic Arabia had been restricted to the tribal system, the novel political structures of the Islamic state at Medina and the subsequent empire could only be *conceived* in Qur'ānic, that is religious, terms.

The conquest of Syria, Egypt, and Iraq in a couple of decades brought the Muslim Arabs into contact with a higher intellectual culture associated chiefly with different forms of the Christian religion. The reactions of the Muslims to this higher culture were in part determined by their earlier experiences at Medina, where the Jewish inhabitants had made fun of some Qur'ānic ideas and assertions. Muḥammad had felt this to be a threat to the very foundation of the religion of Islam, and the

Muslims had adopted a hostile attitude to the Jews. Expansion beyond the frontiers of Arabia led to hostile contacts with Christians. By the time they had become the occupying army in largely Christian lands the Muslims were predisposed to be suspicious of Christian ideas and arguments. Unknown Muslim intellectuals elaborated from hints in the Qur'ān a theory of the 'corruption' (*taḥrīf*) of the Jewish and Christian scriptures.[3] The theory, though complex, was not altogether consistent; but inconsistency was here an advantage. The purpose of the theory was to defend the simple-minded Arab from the desert against the arguments of the more nimble-witted Christian townsmen, and for this purpose inconsistency was no drawback; if one form of the 'corruption' theory failed to parry the Christian criticism, another form would be more successful. In effect the Muslims refused to listen to arguments on Christian premisses on the ground that the 'corruption' of the Bible rendered these arguments invalid. The Christians had therefore to abandon the discussion or argue from Muslim premisses. All this meant that the Muslim Arab remained untroubled in his acceptance of the Qur'ānic world-view.

This could be no more than a temporary expedient, however, since by the end of the seventh century well-educated townsmen in Iraq and the other provinces were becoming Muslims. Such men required a world-view at least as well worked out in detail as the world-view they had previously held. It is in the elaboration of the Qur'ānic ideas into such a world-view that the great achievement of the Muslim scholars is to be seen. To begin with there was little mere borrowing. Their method was rather to begin from the actual beliefs of the Muslim Arabs and to elaborate these in various directions. Sometimes the interest was theoretical or academic, but often there was a practical reason for the elaboration. With the conversion to Islam of many non-Arabs it could no longer be assumed that everyone would understand the Qur'ān. All along some attention had been given to exegesis or interpretation of the text (*tafsīr*). To this a study of Arabic grammar and lexicography had to be added. Lexicography led to the collection and study of old Arabic poetry, since here, it was held, the true meaning of words was to be found. This was further supplemented by material about the history and antiquities of Arabia. Again, since the understanding of a Qur'ānic passage might depend on knowing the circumstances in which it was revealed, there had to be some study of Muḥammad's career (*sīra*) and his expeditions (*maghāzī*).

In this way the relatively simple world-view of the Qur'ān began to expand and to be surrounded by a whole series of scholarly disciplines which have been called the 'Arabic humanities'. This was not all, however. Poetry, which had deep roots in Arab tradition, continued to be cultivated; and to poetry belles-lettres was added. In due course, as already mentioned, there came into being a vast corpus of Traditions or anecdotes about Muḥammad; and this produced a new group of disciplines which had a prominent place in the Islamic world-view. Scholars had not merely to memorize the Traditions, but also to study the critique of their authenticity and the biographies of their transmitters. Jurisprudence, as already mentioned, was in some ways the crown of the Islamic intellectual edifice. Besides the study of the details of legal practice attention was given to legal theory under the rubric of 'the roots of law'. Supplementary to this to a slight extent, and also of practical importance for administrative purposes, besides being of intrinsic interest, was the study of the history of the caliphate or Islamic empire. Geography was later added. In this way, without taking anything from external sources, there was provided for Muslims a well-furnished intellectual world.

In addition there was some borrowing from the previous cultures of the Islamic heartlands; but this borrowing was rigorously controlled and not allowed to dominate or even greatly modify the essential Qur'ānic world-view.

The numerous conversions from Christianity to Islam made it necessary to have something more positive than the defensive theory of 'corruption' of the Bible. In due course much Biblical material was accepted by Muslims, but practically all of this was material which expanded stories already alluded to in the Qur'ān. There was no interest in the parts of the Bible not mentioned in the Qur'ān. The same was true of Christian historical traditions. In his large universal history Ibn-al-Athīr (d. 1234) gives more space to the story of Joseph (to which sura 12 of the Qur'ān is devoted) than to the whole history of the Roman empire. The Muslims had access to Christian historical works, but considered that the actions of *dhimmīs* ('protected persons') or 'infidels' were of no significance. Ibn-al-Athīr contents himself with giving a list of the emperors and the length of their reigns–something useful to the Muslim for chronological purposes. More was taken from the Persian historical tradition, doubtless because the Persians had been incorporated in the Islamic community, and in the running of the empire many lessons had been taken over from Persian statesmanship (but this topic is the concern of the next chapter).

Also of great interest is the way in which certain aspects of the Greek intellectual tradition were incorporated into the Islamic world-view. Translations from Greek science and philosophy were made in the early ninth century, probably as the result of a practical interest in medicine and astrology. A group of Islamic theologians known as the Muʿtazilites then found it convenient to use Greek concepts and arguments in their defence of Islam against internal and external opponents. These concepts and arguments came to be accepted by many strands of Islamic thought. A form of Neoplatonism partly adapted to the Islamic environment is expounded in the works of al-Fārābī (d. 950) and Avicenna (or Ibn-Sīnā; d. 1037). This was regarded as heretical and was not generally accepted; but their logic and some of their metaphysical conceptions were introduced by al-Ghazālī (d. 1111) into the main stream of Sunnite theology, and thus became part of the Islamic 'Bildungsgut'. Since by the eleventh and twelfth centuries much Greek science had also been assimilated, the great Islamic scholars, thinkers and scientists had reached the highest spheres of intellectual life, and were superior to the intellectuals of Christendom at this period. Thus the intellectual efforts of the religious institution of Islam over the centuries had led to the Islamic world-view with all its supporting disciplines replacing and improving on the Christian and other intellectual cultures of the Middle East.

In what has already been said some insight has been given into the ways in which this came about. Much was due to the self-confidence of the Arabs which made them so fully assured of the truth of their own views and unable to see any value in those of other people. On the one hand they insisted on presenting their own material and taking it as the basis of discussions on all topics. On the other hand they neglected alternative views. By asserting that the Bible was 'corrupt' they forced Christians to argue with them on Islamic ground; and they showed no interest in the achievements of Christians in the Roman empire. Complementing this neglect of others was their 'hidden borrowing', that is, their appropriation of non-Islamic material without acknowledgement. Much of the old wisdom of the Middle East was attributed to Muḥammad in the form of Traditions. Muslim scholars soon recognized that many Traditions were not authentic; but once a Tradition of this kind has gained currency, it is difficult to suppress it, and so even Traditions known to be spurious by some scholars tended to be widely repeated and to be accepted.

If some objectionable view or piece of information was widely disseminated among Muslims, then, before it could be consigned to neglect, it had to be refuted. Great care was taken, in the course of refutation, not to disseminate such a view further. The celebrated jurist Aḥmad ibn-Ḥanbal (d. 855) criticized a friend who, in writing a refutation of the Muʿtazilites (whom both regarded as heretics), had prefaced his arguments against them with a careful statement of their views; at this Aḥmad ibn-Ḥanbal remarked that, for all one knew, some people might read the exposition but not go on to the refutation. This is a piece of insight which is familiar to modern propagandists.[4]

While it is difficult to know how much of the process of forming an Islamic world-view was deliberately planned, there is no doubt that it was eminently successful. Among the Muslims there were views which flourished for a time, which in favourable circumstances contributed something of value to the common store, and which then faded away completely. Where any non-Islamic ideas managed to spring up, they faded away even more rapidly, or else were preserved by a dwindling circle of people. Even those 'protected minorities' which stubbornly refused conversion were influenced by the Islamic world-view. The vast structure of Islamic thought was thus intellectually dominant in the culture of the Middle East. It may be that this dominance was no greater than that of Catholic Christianity in Western Europe during the Middle Ages, but it was achieved against much better equipped rivals than had existed in Western Europe.

3. The religious institution and the rulers

From the time of its recognition by the ʿAbbāsids soon after they came to power the religious institution was in a weak position. The appointments open to the ulema, the members of the religious institution, were almost all made by the rulers. If a man wanted to obtain the post of judge, he must be careful not to offend those who wielded political authority; there appear to have been usually more candidates for posts than there were posts. The subservience to which this situation led is illustrated by what happened in the so-called 'Inquisition' or Miḥna from 833 to 849. For reasons to be explained more fully in the next chapter it was decreed in 833 that the chief officials in the capital and the provinces had to make a public declaration that they accepted the theological doctrine of the createdness of the Qur'ān. Although not many actually believed this doctrine, the great majority made the declaration; they had no conviction sufficient to nerve them to endure the loss of a post and other material hardships which would have followed on refusal. Some scholars have pointed out that, when the *waqf* (religious trust) system expanded, this gave many of the ulema a measure of independence, since they could gain a livelihood from the administration of trust properties.[5] Despite this mitigation, however, the fundamental weakness remained.

It was the condition of weakness which probably led to the increasing rigidity of the legal system. One of the obvious dangers was that the rulers would bring pressure to bear on the judge in certain cases in order to gain a decision in their favour. As the law grew more complex, the loopholes for such conduct probably increased, and it would often be easy to find a compliant jurist. In time, however, judges became more bound by precedents. The right of *ijtihād* or 'independent judgement', that is, the working out of a decision from general principles, was restricted, and the phrase came to be used that 'the gate of *ijtihād* had been closed'. The date of this closure is sometimes placed as early as AD 900, but other evidence suggests a date at least two centuries later.[6] While this meant a loss of flexibility in the law, it was also a defence of judicial proceedings against the rulers. The judge could resist pressure on the grounds that on the point in question the decision was established by precedent and that it was not within his competence to review this decision.

As already mentioned, the religious institution had a rival in the 'secretaries', the various grades of administrators employed directly by the rulers or ruling institution. About 850 with the end of the 'Inquisition' the rulers had decided that, because of general conditions in the empire, they must rely more on the ulema and on the populace supporting them than on the secretaries. For nearly a century after 850 the ulema appear to have flourished, but in 945 Baghdad and the central regions of the empire came under the rule of a dynasty of Shīʿite war-lords, the Buwayhids or Būyids. This was doubtless an important period in the development of the corps of ulema, since they had most of the responsibility for preserving the Sunnite structure of society; and at the same time the Buwayhids were encouraging the formation of Shīʿite ulema. Unfortunately these points have not yet been adequately studied.

The eleventh century saw the decline of the Buwayhids, and in 1055 Baghdad came into the hands of the Sunnite Turkish dynasty of Seljūqs, and for the next century these controlled the central Islamic lands. The Seljūqs came to realize that their power could be greatly increased by the ideological support of the Sunnite ulema, and an understanding, almost an alliance, grew up between the actual rulers and the religious institution. This went further than the understanding between the early ʿAbbāsids and the embryonic religious institution of that time. The important step was due to the initiative of the great vizier, Niẓām-al-Mulk, who about 1070 began to set up colleges–each called after him a *madrasa Niẓāmiyya*–in about a dozen of the chief cities of the empire, including Baghdad. These colleges aimed at giving instruction at the highest possible level in the various disciplines required for the support of the Sunnite form of Islam; and the greatest scholars of the time were professors in them. Not merely was higher education more systematically organized than previously, but the teaching given in these new colleges was accepted as the proper qualification for a career as a 'secretary' in the higher administration of the empire. In short the ulema had triumphed completely over their old rivals the 'secretaries', and from now on the administrative service was filled with men who were roughly of the same social class as the ulema.

With many local variations this established the pattern followed in most Islamic countries until the European impact in the nineteenth and twentieth centuries began to produce changes. It is therefore important to understand both the extent of the achievement of the religious institution and the points at which the ulema yielded to the rulers. The positive achievement was not simply that they gained recognition for their own position, but that there was implied in this a recognition of the control of the structure of society by the Sharīʿa. As a result of this latter recognition the fabric of Islamic society remained virtually unshaken amid the political convulsions of the next few centuries. For a time also the Sharīʿa controlled many other aspects of the life of the ordinary people; but the aspects thus controlled tended to decrease in number, since the rigidity of the Sharīʿa made adaptation to changing circumstances difficult.

From the first, however, there were also elements of failure. The recognition of the religious institution and its teaching by the ʿAbbāsids and later rulers was never complete, never extended to the whole of life. Although in conception the Sharīʿa enshrined the Islamic moral ideal for the whole of life, there were certain areas which in practice it never embraced. This was notably the case in the relationship of the caliph or sultan to his chief ministers; when a vizier's policies became displeasing to the caliph, the vizier might be imprisoned and deprived of his property, or even executed, without the semblance of a trial. The ulema, too, so lacked interest in this area that they made no attempt to apply the principles of the Sharīʿa to it. Again, while the recognition of the religious institution meant that the rulers were unable to modify the Sharīʿa in any way but could only administer it, the rulers were able to extend greatly the area covered by administrative decrees. In the establishment of a court and the appointment of a *qāḍī* or Sharīʿa judge, it was an administrative matter to define the competence of the court and judge; and in the absence of a properly constituted court and judge a particular part of the Sharīʿa could not be applied.

The rulers also developed judicial or quasi-judicial institutions which were not bound by the Sharīʿa or at least not completely bound. One was the office of *muḥtasib* or 'inspector of the markets', thought to be modelled on the Byzantine office of *agoranomos*, but also including a general supervision of public morals. Criminal jurisdiction came to be mainly under the *shurṭā* or police. There was also a form of appeal from the *qāḍī*. This was technically an appeal to the ruler who had appointed the *qāḍī* and who was ultimately responsible for the administration of the Sharīʿa; in practice the ruler appointed a special tribunal known as 'the investigation of complaints' (*naẓar fī-l-maẓālim*), and this came to handle many matters with a measure of freedom from the Sharīʿa.[7] In all these ways the triumph of the religious institution was whittled away in practice. Yet its great achievement remained, the creation of a solidly established order of society.

For the members of the religious institution, or at least the more illustrious of them, the conditions under which they had to work were sometimes far from satisfactory. From the writings of al-Ghazālī (d. 1111)—notably the opening book of his *Revival of the Religious Sciences* and parts of his autobiographical work, *Deliverance from Error*[8]—one gathers that the dominant concern among the ulema of his time was advancement in their careers. This concern so warped their outlook that, when they came to write books, they chose subjects which were of no practical importance but in which they could demonstrate their mastery of scholarly techniques. Al-Ghazālī found this perversion of scholarship and pursuit of wealth and celebrity soul-destroying; in consequence, though appointed at an early age to one of the best professorships in Baghdad, he abandoned it after four years in order to lead a kind of monastic life.

The first manifestations of what might have become a rival religious institution are usually dated about a century after the death of al-Ghazālī. These are the religious orders or dervish orders.[9] From the very beginnings of Islam individual Muslims had adopted an ascetic and mystical life, and sometimes outstanding men (or women) had gathered followers round them. There was a continuous mystical tradition, but no organization of common life had persisted beyond a decade or two. In the early thirteenth century, however, orders began to be organized which have endured to the present century. The appearance of orders at that juncture is probably to be connected with the loss of moral leadership by the ulema, and even more with their increasingly close connection with the rulers, for this connection made ordinary people feel that the ulema had taken the side of the rulers against them. The orders certainly gained much popular support, and for many people the ecstatic worship of an order (its *dhikr*) came to mean far more than the formal worship prescribed in the Sharīʿa, the five daily prayers. The full members of the orders were relatively few, but by the nineteenth century most men in the towns and villages of Egypt, for example, were attached to an order and attended its worship or *dhikr*.

The threat of the orders to the established religious institution was effectively met. On the one hand they were given a measure of recognition; this was perhaps chiefly due to the rulers, but the religious institution acceded.[10] The rulers saw clearly that the orders exercised an important function in helping the common people to accept their lot. The partial recognition of the orders made it possible to exercise some control over their more heretical tendencies. On the other hand, the orders were disunited and unable to constitute a single religious institution. Their speculative thinking, too, was often so far removed from the main stream of Islamic intellectual life that it could not flow into this and transform it.[11] Thus the potential new religious institution failed to develop, and by the twentieth century the orders were mostly in decline, and this decline was almost wholly from internal causes. The old religious institution maintained its position in the body politic, but was less and less able to perform its functions, especially since it was unbelievably slow in adapting itself to the circumstances of the nineteenth and twentieth centuries. As will be shown later, it has virtually been replaced by a new body of intellectuals, who do not, however, constitute a religious institution.

SEVEN

THE FORM OF THE POLITICAL STRUGGLE

1. The Persian imperial tradition

The chief purpose of the present chapter is to examine the precise form taken by the political struggle under a strong autocratic government. The period to be specially considered is the ninth century, and an important factor in the struggle was the approval with which many men looked back to the kind of government traditionally associated with the Sasanid Persian dynasty. So before coming to the struggle itself we must glance at the changes brought about during the first half century of ʿAbbāsid rule (750-800). The most important of these changes are comprehended under the rubric of the incorporation of the Persian imperial tradition.

It has already been explained that, up to the year 750, when a non-Arab became a Muslim, he had to become a client or *mawlā* of an Arab tribe. The full members of the tribe looked down on the clients and treated them as inferior beings. Sometimes this might have economic consequences. Especially among some Persians and persianized Aramaeans, whose forebears had participated in the relatively high culture established in Iraq and spreading in Persia, there was intense resentment against Arab arrogance. The ʿAbbāsids' main support seems to have come from clients, though they had also behind them some Arabs of Shīʿite sympathies and most of the general religious movement. Because of the extent of their support from Persians the ʿAbbāsids were bound to go some way towards meeting the aspirations of the clients. The special position of the Arabs came to an end, especially through the disappearance of the stipend system. The new emphasis on the Sharīʿa or revealed law of Islam doubtless helped. Islam is essentially a universalist religion in which all the believers are brothers on a footing of equality; and the privileged status of the Arab Muslim was an 'innovation' which had crept in unperceived.

Pure Arabism had also shown itself deficient in political conceptions for the running of an empire. The ruler of vast territories cannot allow persons without responsibilities to obstruct effective action, for this was what had tended to happen to the Umayyad caliphs when they consulted a council of leading Arab Muslims. There are indications that the Umayyads were beginning to be interested in Persian forms of government.[1] With the coming to power of the ʿAbbāsids Persian influence rapidly increased, especially since the removal of the capital to Iraq meant that the caliphs were bound to employ as 'secretaries' many persons who had inherited something of the Persian administrative tradition. The most obvious manifestation of the change was that the caliph became difficult of access for the ordinary Muslim, especially through the elaboration of court ceremonial on a Persian pattern. At the same time the class of notables, whether descended from the pre-Islamic Arab aristocracy or from the men of Badr and other early Muslims, had less influence. The caliph was under no obligation to consult them. These notables gradually lost their status as a class and were replaced by a new kind of courtier, largely created by the caliph and dependent on his favour. The new courtiers were mostly men with a gift for administration whom the caliph found useful in the running of the empire. Such men might be rapidly promoted to the highest offices and to great wealth, but might just as rapidly lose everything. Unless their sons were equally gifted they were unlikely to retain the position and privileges of their fathers. Thus through all the centuries of Islamic history from the accession of the ʿAbbāsids in 750 there was little that could be considered a permanent aristocracy. In later times it became common for wealthy men to make some of their property a *waqf* or trust on behalf of their descendants. Although such a trust had a secular purpose, it was protected by a religious sanction, and therefore could not be seized by a rapacious ruler. The disadvantage was that the beneficiaries, though enjoying the rents or other income from the properties, could not use them in any creative way. Nevertheless this practice helped to maintain something of a hereditary upper class.

The development of the office of vizier (Arabic *wazīr*) under the early ʿAbbāsids may be regarded as a result of the acceptance of the Persian tradition. The office took shape gradually, and never had an absolutely fixed form. A rough description would be to say that it was a combination of the modern European offices of head of the civil service and prime minister. Where the caliph was strong and competent, as in the early days of the ʿAbbāsids, the vizier would tend to be the chief civil servant; but if the caliph was weak and incompetent, the vizier would be the real ruler of the empire.[2] One of the contributions of the well-known Barmakids (Barmecides) or family of Barmak was that they discovered, trained and found appointments for a number of bright young 'secretaries', and thus greatly increased the efficiency of the civil service.[3] Training seems to have been given chiefly in the course of ordinary work by a kind of apprenticeship; but suitable recruits normally came from among the sons of 'secretaries', who alone would have the necessary background education. Thus the 'secretaries' were an almost hereditary class. Within the class, however, it was possible for a specially competent man to rise to high office. In 936 the ʿAbbāsid caliphs lost all their political power, and the caliphate was divided into a number of virtually independent states, each of which might have a vizier. No points of principle arise, however. Later Muslim writers assume an identity between the early ʿAbbāsid vizierate and a Sasanid office; but the latter was mainly that of a counsellor. The vizierate is connected with the Persian tradition, however, in that it is derived from the autocratic character of the caliphal power.

Sasanian Persia, of course, was itself the heir of traditions of rule going back for millennia to Sumer and Akkad. An important link in the chain of transmission was the Achaemenian empire of Darius and Xerxes. Thus in adopting the Persian tradition the Muslims were taking over the quintessence of the political experience of the Middle East. In itself this is something that might have been expected. What is interesting and significant, however, is the contrast between the readiness of the Muslims to accept the Persian tradition and their refusal to borrow—or at least to acknowledge any borrowing—from the classical Greek tradition or the Roman and Byzantine tradition. Even those who accepted Greek philosophy paid relatively little attention to the political thought of Plato and Aristotle. A few works, like *Al-madīna al-fāḍila* of al-Fārābī (d. 950) which could be called a Neoplatonic version of Plato's *Republic*, show Greek influence, but they did not appreciably affect the main stream of Islamic political activity. Likewise the Roman-Byzantine empire received cursory treatment from the Muslim historians. The Muslims regarded this as something alien and inferior.

Stories of the Persian, especially Sasanid, kings, on the other hand, came to be quite prominent in certain types of Islamic literature, Arabic as well as Persian. The introduction of Persian themes into Arabic literature is mainly the work of a 'secretary' known as Ibn-al-Muqaffaʿ, who was executed as a heretic in 757. He produced elegant Arabic versions of Persian works, thereby making an important contribution to the development of Arabic prose style. His best known work is *Kalīla wa-Dimna*, or the fables of the Indian sage Bidpai, in which much traditional wisdom, some of a political character, is put into the mouths of animals. He also wrote *The Lives of the Persian Kings* and *The Book of the Crown*, which is said to have been about the life of king Anūshirvān (reigned 531-79).[4] The pro-Persian and anti-Arab attitude of Ibn-al-Muqaffaʿ may have had something to do with his condemnation. Nevertheless just as the Persians were accepted along with the Arabs as full citizens of the caliphate, so Persian history was given a full treatment in universal histories like that of aṭ-Ṭabarī.

Stories about the Persian kings came to be an important ingredient in a new literary genre, and indeed helped to create it. This genre is sometimes known as 'Mirrors for Princes', and in Arabic literature forms a branch of *adab* or belles-lettres. Such works contain good advice on the art of ruling, sometimes based on ethical principles but more often on mere expediency. Sometimes the writers are men with practical experience of ruling; sometimes they are literary figures with little or no experience. In neither case, however, do they attempt to give a systematic political theory.[5] The most interesting and accessible books of this kind are in fact written in Persian. In 1082 a minor prince called Kay Kā'ūs wrote the *Qābūsnāmeh* for his son, and this has been translated into English by Reuben Levy under the title of *A Mirror for Princes.*[6] About the same time Niẓām-al-Mulk (d. 1092), the great vizier of the Seljūqs, wrote the *Siyāsat-nāmeh* at the request of his sovereign; the translation by Hubert Darke is entitled *The Book of Government or Rules for Kings.*[7] Yet a third work from the same period is also available in English, namely *Counsel for Kings* by al-Ghazālī (d. 1111), a theologian associated with Niẓām-al-Mulk, who is said to have written this work a year or so before his own death.[8] Another recent translation is that into French by Charles Pellat of the earlier Arabic *Book of the Crown* attributed falsely to al-Jāhiẓ and written between 847 and 861.[9]

2. The power struggle under the first ʿAbbāsids

The writings of Ibn-al-Muqaffaʿ which have just been mentioned mark the beginning of an all-pervasive struggle for power which filled the first century of ʿAbbāsid rule. It is best regarded as a struggle between rival blocs, since on each side there were a number of different interest-groups. Though the main active struggle came to an end with the 'establishment of Sunnism' about 850, traces of the opposing concepts remain to the present day.

Ibn-al-Muqaffaʿ is a representative of the 'secretaries'. The men of this class in Iraq were often descendants of those who had been employed as 'secretaries' by the Sasanids. At first they had simply been retained by the Muslim governors without any demands except loyalty. In the later Umayyad period, however, the rulers insisted that all 'secretaries' should be Muslims; and most of the hereditary class complied with this demand in externals, though without any great inner conviction. The transference of the seat of government from Syria to Iraq by the ʿAbbāsids meant that these men now had appointments in the central administration of the empire and not merely in a provincial administration. With the adoption of Persian methods of rule by the ʿAbbāsids the hereditary 'secretaries' saw an opportunity of greatly increasing their power as a class–indeed an opportunity of gaining the chief power in the empire. This is part of the reason why Ibn-al-Muqaffaʿ was keen to extol Persian royal achievements and the virtues of Persian statecraft.

On the same side as the 'secretaries' there was also a Persian element. This may in part have coincided with the 'secretaries' but was also in part distinct. At this period there was probably no unified Persian consciousness – the creation of a common awareness of being Iranian is generally attributed to Firdawsī with his epic the *Shāhnāmeh* about the year 1000. Nevertheless there were especially in Iraq both Persians and persianized Aramaeans, all now Muslims, who believed that their previous culture had been superior to that of the Arabs. They felt this all the more because of the arrogance of the Arabs and because of their insistence that non-Arabs on becoming Muslims should be enrolled as clients (*mawālī*) of Arab tribes. The Khorasanian clients in particular had had a large hand in bringing the ʿAbbāsids to power, and did indeed find they had an increasing influence in the affairs of the empire. One way in which this Persian element expressed itself was through the Shuʿūbite movement.[10] This was essentially a literary movement in whose writings non-Arabs and especially Persians were praised and the faults and weaknesses of the Arabs emphasized. Material for the latter was easily found in the Arabs' own poetry, since one class of poem was the 'satire' in which a poet made the most of any real or alleged shameful episodes in the life of the tribes which were enemies of his own tribe. Another feature expressed in the lives of some of the Persian group was a form of asceticism; but this was severely suppressed by ʿAbbāsid rulers under the name of 'irreligion' (*zandaqa*), presumably because it appeared to be a resurgence of Zoroastrian dualism.

Finally in the same bloc there were many men of Shīʿite sympathies. The movement which brought the ʿAbbāsids to power had had considerable support from such persons, but many of them became disillusioned when it turned out that the hitherto unnamed leader – 'him of the family who shall be approved' – was not a descendant of ʿAlī but an ʿAbbāsid. Something has already been said about the origins of Shīʿism (Chapter 3, section 4), and what it meant in practice will have to be considered presently (section 3 below). Here it is to be noticed that there was apparently a large body of Shīʿite opinion, and that the caliphs and their viziers made great efforts to gain the active approval of this body. Along with the 'secretaries' and the Persian element these Shīʿites constituted what will here be called the autocratic bloc.

In the opposite camp the group that in some ways corresponded to the 'secretaries' were the ulema. As a group their power was growing. The ʿAbbāsids had had the support of the general religious movement, and in return gave them certain privileges. The growth of the religious institution constituted by the ulema has already been described. The institution was busy formulating truly Islamic ideals for daily life; and as it achieved this it seems to have had the bulk of the population behind it. This relationship of the ulema to the ordinary people, especially in the cities, was an important factor in the stability of the empire. In so far as the ulema themselves supported the government they were usually able to gain the support of the ordinary people for the government.

Among the opponents of the autocratic bloc two complexes of interest can be distinguished in addition to the class interest of the ulema. The persons moved by these complexes of interest may be much the same as the ulema and their supporters among the ordinary people, but there was certainly a distinction in the dominant interest. Some were chiefly moved by the belief that Arab culture was superior to Persian. Such persons were presumably of pure Arab descent or else descendants of non-Arab clients for whom the process of arabization had been specially meaningful and who had identified themselves with their new ethnic allegiance. The second complex of interest was that which contrasted with Shīʿism and may be called Sunnism, though in the early ninth century men were only beginning to be aware of this as a distinctive attitude. The phrases which came to be used were 'the people of the Sunna (or example of Muḥammad)' and 'the people of the Sunna and the community' (*Ahl as-Sunna*, *Ahl as-Sunna wa-l-jamāʿa*). These Sunnites derived their name from their insistence that the life and activity of the community of Muslims should be based on the Sunna or example of Muḥammad as enshrined in Tradition. Acceptance of Qur'ānic precepts was implied, but the Sunna of Muḥammad was also taken to have a certain revelatory quality, so that Qur'ān and Sunna together determined the Sharīʿa or 'revealed law'.

In effect the Sunnites were demanding that the life of the

empire should be based on the revealed-law. Most of them also thought of the Islamic community as a charismatic one because it was based on this divinely given law, and this conception–as indicated in the discussion of the Khārijites–goes back to an attitude towards the tribe found among many Arabs. The ulema were, of course, the accredited exponents of the divine law. Thus the three complexes of interest, though distinct, are closely linked. For the three the designation of 'constitutionalist bloc' seems appropriate.[11]

The detailed working out of the struggle cannot be described here. At least from the time of Hārūn ar-Rashīd (786-809), however, the caliphs were searching for a solid basis for their power. Hārūn himself in the Barmakid period (up to 803) was relying mainly on the support of the autocratic bloc, but there was discontent among the constitutionalists; and the fall of the Barmakids initiated an attempt to appease the latter. Most of the caliphate of al-Ma'mūn was spent in trying to find a compromise; and the policy of the Inquisition (to be examined presently), which lasted from 833 to about 849, was the culmination of a series of experiments. The ending of the policy of the Inquisition early in the reign of al-Mutawakkil was an admission of its failure; and this was followed by a decision to rely mainly on the constitutionalist bloc. From this time onwards the Islamic empire was predominantly Sunnite, even when temporal power was wielded by Shīʿite war-lords. The second half of the ninth century and the early tenth century were the decades when the hitherto fluid intellectual basis of the empire received the definite forms which it has retained ever since. Such processes as the formation of the canon of sound Tradition, the recording of permissible variations in the reciting of the Qur'ān and the inauguration of the intellectualist schools of Sunnite theology (Ashʿarite and Māturīdite) may together be described as 'the establishment of Sunnism'.

3. The intellectual form of the struggle

The struggle between the autocratic and constitutionalist blocs was fought out at many levels. This is true of all such struggles, of course. It is specially important, however, for occidental students to understand the precise nature of the intellectual, ideological or ideational aspect of the struggle. Ultimately this will be seen to be similar to parts of European political thought; but the similarity is not at first obvious, and some consideration of this aspect is therefore fruitful. In particular two sets of ideas will be studied, historical and theological.

(a) *Historical.* In the lists of Arabic works written in the ninth century the modern scholar finds a number of titles concerning the first two or three decades of Islamic history following the death of Muḥammad. The unwary tiro might deduce that this meant that there was an upsurge in the interest in history as we understand it in the twentieth century. This was not so, however. There was no widespread interest of an academic kind. On the contrary, the writers of the books and pamphlets had a vital concern in their contemporary politics. If they could show that before Muḥammad died in 632–nearly two hundred years earlier!–ʿAlī had been designated his successor, and that therefore Abū-Bakr, ʿUmar and ʿUthmān were interlopers, they would have greatly strengthened the case for Shīʿism and reliance on the autocratic bloc. Further, if it was true that ʿAlī had been thus designated, then it could be inferred that the proper method for the appointment of the imam (as the Shīʿites preferred to call the head of state instead of caliph) was designation by his predecessor. This became the essential basis of his rule, and no place was left for the people's *bayʿa*, their acknowledgement and oath of allegiance.[12]

Some of the accounts which have come down to us about the attitudes of the Shīʿites in the ninth century make it appear that they were revolutionaries plotting for the overthrow of the ʿAbbāsid régime. This is because later Shīʿite writers have a list of twelve imams stretching from ʿAlī down to the year 874 when the twelfth disappeared. From the claim that ʿAlī was the rightful imam in 632 and that he transmitted the imamate down the line of twelve, it seems to follow that, up to 874, those who insisted on the claim of ʿAlī must have held that his successor at any given date was the rightful ruler of the Islamic empire. This conclusion must be false, however, for the men in question were known to the ʿAbbāsids and received no harsher treatment than being placed in 'protective custody'; sometimes they were at liberty. Had they been actively plotting, this must have become known to the ʿAbbāsids and the plotters would have been put to death. From these considerations it can be seen that many aspects of the history of Islam from 632 onwards became relevant to political discussions in the ninth and tenth centuries, and care is needed to distinguish genuine historical materials from the rewriting of such material by political pamphleteers. A Danish scholar has recently made a valuable study of the effect of political attitudes on the writing of the history of the period from 656 to 661.[13] In the case of the line of ʿAlid imams under the ʿAbbāsids it would seem that they were recognized as heads of the family during their lifetime, but not as anything more than this.

In other societies also, of course, history has been the basis of contemporary political claims. One thinks of the place in European history of the so-called Donation of Constantine. Yet in the Islamic world there seems to have been rather more of this, with greater concentration on arguments for and against a relatively small number of assertions. Thus a distinguished writer of the ninth century, al-Jāḥiẓ (d. 868), wrote a defence of the (not adequately studied) political sect of the ʿUthmānites (ʿUthmāniyya), but the whole book of some two hundred pages consists of arguments to show that Abū-Bakr was superior to ʿAlī.[14] There is thus justification for the assertion that historical discussions are part of the intellectual form of the political struggle.

(b) *Theological.* To the average modern reader it is unthinkable that the question whether the Qur'ān is the uncreated speech of God or the created speech of God should be a political one. Yet shortly before his death in 833 the caliph al-Ma'mūn decreed that senior officials in Baghdad and the provincial capitals should publicly profess their belief in the doctrine of the createdness of the Qur'ān. Most did so, some uneasily, but a few refused and were ready to endure the sufferings involved. Notable among these was the jurist Aḥmad ibn-Ḥanbal. This imposition of a public profession of belief is known as the Inquisition or Miḥna.[15] The policy was officially continued, though not always vigorously carried out, until the beginning of the reign of al-Mutawakkil about 848 or 849. The ending of the policy was probably not due to the resistance of a few men like Ibn-Ḥanbal but to general considerations, especially the realization that the constitutionalist bloc would give the most satisfactory basis for the régime.

The political relevance of this theological doctrine will become clear if one looks at it in relation to the struggle between the two blocs. At the heart of this struggle was the rivalry between the ulema and the 'secretaries'. The ulema and their supporters believed that the state should be governed in accordance with the Sharīʿa, that is, the law implicit in the Qur'ān and the Traditions. This gave the ulema considerable power in the affairs of the empire, since they were the recognized exponents of the Sharīʿa. On the other hand, the 'secretaries' held that the good government of the empire depended on the charisma of the leader or head of state. Now if the Qur'ān was created, God could presumably have created a different Qur'ān in other circumstances. Or – to put the same point in a different way – God's plenipotentiary, the imam or charismatic head of state, acting with divine authority, could set aside (or declare 'abrogated') specific commands of the Qur'ān and, more generally, the provisions of the Sharīʿa. The alternative doctrine, however, namely, that the Qur'ān was the uncreated speech of God, implied that the Qur'ān was an essential part of the being of God; as such none of it could be set aside by any human agent, especially when his charismatic authority was not admitted. Thus the question whether the Qur'ān was created or uncreated closely affected the respective roles in government of the ulema and the 'secretaries'.

The matter was in fact more complex than this. In the reign of al-Ma'mūn there came into prominence a group of theologians known as the Muʿtazilites who made use of Greek philosophical concepts in their intellectual defence of Islamic doctrines. Greek philosophy and science was beginning to be translated into Arabic and was popular in court circles. There the Muʿtazilites also came to have some influence. They were the chief advocates of the doctrine of the createdness of the Qur'ān. Some of them had sympathies with Shīʿism, but they were not Shīʿites. Their doctrine in this respect was rather an attempt at compromise,[16] and it was doubtless as a compromise that it appealed to the caliph and his ministers. It gave some support to the 'secretaries' against the ulema, but did not admit the claims of the Shīʿite imams in any form and so did not wholly undermine the position of the ulema. As might have been foreseen neither party was satisfied. The end of the

Inquisition was a surrender to the constitutionalists, for it was realized that the empire could not continue to exist without the support of the ulema and the masses who followed them. This support was needed not only against the autocratic bloc, but also against the increasingly important Turkish mercenaries.

This is an example of the great political importance of apparently hair-splitting theological doctrines. It may be complemented by a trifling illustration of the way in which political disputes could lead to theological arguments. In the Qur'ān (37.102/0-113) there is a reference to Abraham's readiness to sacrifice his son at God's command, but the name of the son is not mentioned. To the modern occidental scholar this is a simple matter – the son is Isaac. It is a historical point, and we have our 'historical' source, the Bible. The Muslims, however, were less deferential to the Bible, and saw other implications. Ishmael, all agreed, was the ancestor of the Arabs. Isaac came to be regarded by some as the ancestor of the Persians, and even of the Greeks and Romans. So the question 'which of Abraham's sons?' became a question of the relative merits of Arabs and Persians, and was decided mainly on this basis, for it is now generally held by Muslims that the son was Ishmael. In this way theology becomes an aspect of the intellectual form of the political struggle in Islam.

EIGHT

THE COMMUNITY AS BEARER OF VALUES

1. The nature and purpose of the community

In endeavouring to describe further what is implied in the 'establishment of Sunnism' we must turn to think once again in a general way about the community. In particular we have to think about the phrase sometimes used of the main body of the Muslims, namely, that it is a 'sect attaining safety or bringing salvation' (*firqa nājiya*). This is tantamount to saying that it is as a member of the Islamic community that a man achieves meaning or significance in his life or realizes genuine values. In all this the Islamic community or *umma* was taking the place, on a much vaster scale, of the pre-Islamic nomadic tribe. The nomad gave a prominent place to the conception of the tribe as a bearer of values, though he expressed this, of course, in his own way. His poets extolled the noble deeds performed by the tribe according to the ideal of 'fortitude' (*ḥamāsa*), which a modern writer has defined as including 'bravery in battle, patience in misfortune, persistence in revenge, protection of the weak and defiance of the strong'.[1] The capacity for performing noble deeds was held to be carried by the tribal stock; and so, if a man achieved something noble, it was because of the tribal blood in his veins. It was largely to the military strength of the tribe, too, that he owed his preservation from physical danger and the possibility of gaining food and shelter. Many of his actions were motivated by a zealous desire to maintain the honour of the tribe.

Perhaps the original reluctance of the Muslim Arabs to accord to non-Arabs all the privileges they themselves enjoyed was due to a transference of this feeling of nobility from particular tribes to the body of Arab Muslims as a whole. When the

'Abbāsid dynasty came to power in 750 it was pledged to remove the grievances of the 'clients' or non-Arab Muslims, and in practice this meant basing the conduct of affairs on strictly Islamic principles. These were to be found primarily in the Qur'ān and secondarily in the Sunna or standard practice of Muḥammad. The principles derived from these sources constituted the Sharī'a or revealed-law. The 'tribe' of Muslims had, of course, no nobility of tribal stock, but in its possession of the divinely-given Sharī'a it had a claim to nobility of another kind. The Sharī'a, moreover, showed the individual Muslim what acts to perform and to avoid in order to merit Heaven and in this way gave him the possibility of attaining 'salvation'. The Islamic community thus performed for its members many of the functions performed by the nomadic tribe. The caliph or other ruler had always the duty of maintaining internal and external peace and security, and this was taken to imply the maintenance of conditions which would make it possible for a man to worship God according to the Sharī'a.

From shortly after the time of its establishment at Medina the Islamic state was expanding, and this expansion continued with some breaks for at least a hundred years after Muḥammad's death. Because of this certain political concepts presuppose expansion, and indeed expansion that in the end will be world-wide. This is expressed by the distinction between 'the sphere of Islam' and 'the sphere of war' (*dār al-islām*, *dār al-ḥarb*). Territories where the ruler is a Muslim and the life of the people is based on the Sharī'a constitute 'the sphere of Islam', whereas all other territories are 'the sphere of war'. These concepts are closely associated with that of the *jihād* or holy war. They are not really applicable to the foreign policy of a large state with vast territories. In practice, of course, a Muslim ruler did not inaugurate a holy war against non-Muslim neighbours unless he had a good prospect of success, and indeed it was his duty not to do so. Thus more and more the distinction between the two spheres became irrelevant in practice, though it continued to have a place in political theorizing. It was also discussed whether there could be a third sphere, the sphere of truce; but even those jurists who admitted a third sphere confined it to truces with non-Muslims who acknowledged Muslim suzerainty.[2] There is thus little place for a treaty on equal terms between an Islamic state and a non-Islamic, though juristic ingenuity brought this under the heading of giving 'protection' or a 'guarantee of security' to an enemy.[3] Nevertheless a belief in the final supremacy of Islam tends to be implicit in any such agreements.

As one looks back over the past history of the Islamic world the first impression is that these concepts have become largely theoretical and had less and less effect on practice. The original idea of the *jihād* was useful in Arabian conditions, and indeed while the Islamic state was expanding rapidly, but was not a sufficient basis for the foreign policy of an empire; and the same would seem to be true of the related concepts of 'the sphere of Islam' and 'the sphere of war'. Yet this first impression is in part misleading. The Ottoman diplomats negotiating the treaty of Karlowitz in 1699 were psychologically unprepared for a situation in which they were the defeated party and their territories were being reduced; all that was happening was contrary to their basic assumptions. More recently the position of Pakistan within the British Commonwealth has been affected by the concept of 'the sphere of Islam'; the theory accepted by other members that the Queen was the nominal head of each state and that the actual head of state acted in her name was unthinkable in Pakistan, since it would have meant an Islamic state with a non-Muslim head. It was, of course, easy for Pakistanis to agree on this point since, besides being traditional, it had little bearing on practice, unlike other differences of opinion on how to make Pakistan a truly Islamic and yet modern state.[4]

The correct conclusion to be drawn from such observations is probably that the traditional political concepts are still alive as ideals, and that Muslims put them into practice wherever they are able. In many aspects of politics, however, the difficulties are immense and no solution has yet been found. What is the Islamic basis for becoming members of international bodies like the United Nations? What is to be the attitude of a Muslim who lives in a mainly non-Muslim country like India? In this connection, however, it is well to remember that many Christians make similar optimistic assumptions about the future of Christianity, even though their assumptions have a less precise political content.

2. Ideals and laws

The decision of the caliphal government or ruling institution shortly before 850 that it would rely primarily on the ulema and the masses who supported them led among other things to the fixing of the canon of 'sound Tradition'. The two main collections of 'sound Traditions', known simply as 'the Sound' (*aṣ-Ṣaḥīḥ*), are those of al-Bukhārī (d. 870) and Muslim (d. 875); and these were followed by four more collections, also regarded as canonical, whose authors died between 886 and 915.[5] These collections were made after a critique of the innumerable anecdotes current about Muḥammad and the rejection of a great many as 'unsound'. Modern historical criticism holds that the criteria employed by the Muslim critics were insufficient; but this judgement, though in one respect correct, is based on the false assumption that the Muslim scholars were trying to attain historical objectivity. It would be more accurate to say that they were trying to give a concrete expression to the values on which the life of the Islamic community was founded.

As has already been explained, the Traditions now collected and accepted as canonical were anecdotes about what Muḥammad had said or done on certain occasions. The complete Tradition included the names of those who had transmitted the Tradition. For Muslim scholars the test of the authenticity of the Tradition was primarily whether all the persons mentioned in the chain of transmission were men of sound political and theological views. The important question for the modern student thus becomes: 'What is the function of the Muslim critique of Traditions?' When the question is put in this form, it is seen that the Muslim scholars were trying to eliminate all eccentric views, and at the same time to give concrete expression to the values and ideals accepted by the main body of the ulema and other intellectuals. In other words the corpus of sound Traditions enshrines the values and ideals accepted by the main body of Sunnite Muslims about the year 850. It was natural that Muḥammad should be accepted as an exemplar and model, but this acceptance probably only became widespread after the great jurist ash-Shāfiʿī (d. 820) insisted that all legal decisions, where there was no prescription in the Qur'ān, should be based on a Tradition going back to Muḥammad himself. There were probably a few genuine reminiscences of Muḥammad, and a relatively clear picture of the *kind* of person he had been; and this picture would control any modification or even invention of anecdotes. In this way the Traditions had an authentic basis, and yet there was a potentiality of adaptation to the conditions of Baghdad in the middle ninth century–so different from those of early seventh-century Mecca and Medina.

The Traditions were not collected for historical but for legal purposes. Together with the Qur'ān they–or rather the 'standard practice' (Sunna) of the Prophet which they described–were the basis of the Sharīʿa or revealed-law of Islam. Although the term 'law' is used, the Sharīʿa is not comparable to modern legislation. It is essentially an ideal law. Indeed it is an ideal code of conduct with a much wider scope than any modern legislation, since it also includes matters of hygiene, etiquette and the ritual of worship. So far as the present study is concerned, only those aspects of the Sharīʿa will be considered which are dealt with by contemporary legislation.

The most important feature of the Sharīʿa to be noted here is that it is a divinely given law. Because of this it cannot be altered by any human legislator. The only human control of the Sharīʿa is through interpretation, and interpretation is taken to include the application of the principles of the Sharīʿa to novel circumstances. The only authorized interpreters of the Sharīʿa are the ulema, as already explained; and even in their case it is debated whether they have a right of independent interpretation (*ijtihād*) or are bound by precedents (*taqlīd*). It is admitted even in respect of the Qur'ān itself–by the doctrine of 'abrogation' (*an-nāsikh wa-l-mansūkh*)–that the application of general principles varies according to circumstances. Thus the Sharīʿa may be said to correspond to human nature. Basically, however, the general principles are divinely given and eternal. They are commands which man cannot change, but can only obey or disobey.

Though the Islamic ruler has, strictly speaking, no power of legislating, he is not purely passive with regard to the Sharīʿa. The ruler has always been regarded as having power to appoint judges and to define their sphere of responsibility. The sphere is usually restricted geographically, but it may also be limited with regard to the type of case; e.g. for a particular judge commercial contracts may be excluded from his competence, or it may be limited to questions of personal status. By such administrative decisions a ruler may prevent many aspects of the Sharīʿa from being applied in his dominions. In modern times this principle has been used by governments to bring about reforms which would have been difficult otherwise. Thus in some countries courts were bothered with claims for alimony based on pregnancies allegedly lasting up to four years; the possibility of such lengthy pregnancies could not simply be denied without raising difficult questions about the reliability of historical sources, since some cases were recorded from early Islamic times. So a government would simply decree that judges were not to hear cases in which a pregnancy of longer than a year was alleged.[6] In general it may be said that by the late nineteenth century, as a result of the power of rulers to define the competency of courts and judges, little of the Sharīʿa was being applied in the most progressive Islamic countries apart from sections dealing with personal status (marriage, divorce and inheritance).

Despite the theory that the ruler had no legislative power rulers came to issue decrees that were tantamount to legislation and to establish courts which were not bound by the Sharīʿa. The courts began to appear in the early Islamic period. There were police courts which, when there was no Qur'ānic punishment for a crime, dealt with criminals according to local custom. Then there was the court of the *muḥtasib*, an official who is said to have taken the place of the Byzantine *agoranomos* or inspector of markets, but who developed into a general censor of public morals. Still more important was the ruler's prerogative of 'investigating complaints' (*an-naẓar fī-l-maẓālim*)–a part of the Persian imperial tradition taken over by the ʿAbbāsids (and perhaps by the later Umayyads). This was essentially a function of the ruler as supreme judicial authority. The 'complaints' might be against a judge or other official; but more and more they came to be concerned with matters which had not been submitted to the Sharīʿa courts, presumably because these were found to be in some way unsatisfactory. In these ways the theory that the Sharīʿa applied to the whole of life was greatly modified in practice.[7]

The issuing of legislative decrees grew out of the necessity of making administrative decisions. The dividing line between legislation and administrative decisions of a general nature is a fine one. It would seem, too, that in many administrative matters the ulema made no attempt to elaborate rules of what would be in accordance with the Sharīʿa–they were neither interested in this nor had they the practical experience needed. For these reasons the practice developed of formulating administrative decisions as general rules. The practice was greatly extended under the Ottoman empire, and such a rule was called a *qānūn.*[8] The theory was that each *qānūn* was in accordance with the Sharīʿa and an application of its general provisions, but actually some were opposed to the Sharīʿa. The attempt was sometimes made to give a theoretical justification of the issuing of rules by governments; it was emphasized that every Muslim had a duty, so far as he could act effectively, 'to command the good and forbid the evil' (*al-amr bi-l-maʿrūf wa-n-nahy ʿan al-munkar*), but that this was specially incumbent on the caliph or other ruler in virtue of his authority and power.[9]

3. The community and the individual

The basic purpose of government is to give the community of Muslims internal and external security so that each may be able to gain a livelihood for himself and his dependants and to carry out his religious duties, especially that of worship. It is significant that in Islamic political thinking there is virtually no mention of the rights of man nor of the concept of freedom. With regard to the question of rights, it is of course the case that a Muslim may justifiably expect other Muslims to act in certain ways towards him and to refrain from certain acts. These are not thought of, however, as rights belonging to the individual; the emphasis is rather on the fact that God has commanded the others to act, or refrain from acting, in these ways.[10]

Similarly the concept of freedom has never had any place in Islamic political thought. There is a word for 'freedom', namely *ḥurriyya*, but this refers to the condition of the free man (*ḥurr*) as contrasted with the slave (*ʿabd*). A recent scholar, after collecting a relatively large amount of material on this topic, stated as his conclusion that, though 'freedom as an ideal was not unknown, as a political force it lacked the support which only a central position within the political organism and system of thought could give it'.[11] Part of the reason for the unimportance of the concept of freedom is doubtless the theological view that man is always the slave (*'abd*) of God; but the matter is one deserving further reflection. It is perhaps worth noting in this connection that Muslims give great prominence to the virtue of 'patience' (*ṣabr*) and that this includes not only the endurance of hardships and ill-treatment but also the acceptance of man's servile status as subject to God's commands. There is also a widespread feeling in the Middle East that some government is better than no government, and that revolution (the overthrow of the existing government) is generally a bad thing. Despite such points, however, it seems likely that there is a combination of ideas somewhere in Islamic thought, which performs much the same function as the concept of freedom does in the West.

Against the occidental principle of *homo homini lupus*–which may be part of the reason for the emphasis on freedom–the Islamic community has a strong sense of brotherhood, and in this respect continues the solidarity of the Arabian tribe. This brotherhood is not just theoretical, but influences the actual conduct of Muslims in many ways. Thus there is no racial discrimination in Islam (after the Arabs accepted the non-Arab Muslims as equals), though there are traces of colour-consciousness in mediaeval Arabic literature. Where the white missionary to Africa was unwilling to have an African wife, the Muslim trader, though white or nearly white, would not hesitate to marry the daughter of an African Muslim.

Despite the strong sense of brotherhood, however, there was often a tension between the individual and the Islamic community or between individualism and communal solidarity. In some passages of the Qur'ān it is insisted that judgement on the Last Day is pronounced on individuals, whereas there are other passages which describe whole communities going to Hell together because of their solidarity in the rejection of God's message. It was noted in Chapter 5 how the Khārijites emphasized the solidarity of the believers. Communal solidarity, however, led to pressure on deviants to make them conform. The pre-Islamic Arabian tribe would expel a member who transgressed certain norms of conduct, especially where his actions involved blood-feuds with other tribes. Before he went to Medina in 622 Muḥammad had been disowned by the chief Abū-Lahab, presumably in an attempt to get him to abandon aspects of his preaching abhorrent to the great merchants. From time to time in Islamic history we find governments using force to make men conform. The case of the Inquisition instituted by al-Ma'mūn in 833 has already been described. The execution of the mystic al-Ḥallāj in 922 is another example of pressure on individual deviance.[12]

The greatest pressure to conform, however, came not from government action but from the sense of the solidarity of the community. In many cases this seems to have made a man *want* to be the same as his fellows and to feel that there was something wrong with him if he behaved or thought differently. To belong to the community meant so much to him – life apart from the community was unthinkable – that everything which threatened to separate him from his fellows was to be avoided. The sense of the solidarity of the community was in part below the level of conceptual awareness. One aspect of it might be formulated in modern terms as a belief in the charismatic nature of the community.[13] Another aspect was expressed by Muslim jurists when they recognized *ijmāʿ* or 'consensus' as a source of the Sharīʿa. The 'consensus' was variously interpreted, and might at one extreme be the agreement of a small body of jurists and at the other that of the whole community of Muslims. The variety indicates an absence of complete conceptualization. In actuality, however, consensus meant the acceptance in theory of what most of the community had accepted in practice.[14] There are weaknesses in the jurists' theory of consensus, but this must not blind the modern student to the strength of communal solidarity as a factor in the development of the Islamic world of today. 'The sense of Muslim solidarity', it has been asserted, 'was a reality independent of the unity or the disunity in the political system'.[15] This sense of solidarity has fostered the integration of many races into the unity of Islam, especially Sunnite Islam, with its tendency towards homogeneity in social and intellectual patterns. The modern statesman neglects this reality at his peril.

NINE

WAR-LORDS AND POLITICAL THEORISTS

1. The emergence of the war-lords

The break-up of the ʿAbbāsid caliphate may be said to have begun in the early ninth century. Already in the eighth century the ʿAbbāsids had failed to assert their authority in Spain, Morocco, and western Algeria, where independent dynasties established themselves. This development, however, did not raise any novel political principles. There was indeed a problem with the Umayyad dynasty in Spain since they were Sunnites who did not recognize the caliph in Baghdad; but the problem led to no wide discussion. The other rulers were Shīʿite and Khārijite sectarians. Novelty is generally held to have appeared when the first of the Aghlabid dynasty was given Tunisia as a hereditary governorship just before 800.[1] The new principle appears most clearly in the case of the distinguished general Ṭāhir, who had been made governor of eastern Persia by al-Ma'mūn; about 821 he began to assert his independence of the caliph, and on his death in 822 al-Ma'mūn recognized his son as his successor to the governorship. The Ṭāhirid dynasty maintained their virtually independent rule until 873, each new ruler receiving a letter of appointment from the ʿAbbāsid caliph of the day. Their rule came to an end not by any action of the caliph but through defeat by a military leader who created a state for himself in Afghanistan and then advanced against the Ṭāhirids. The caliph recognized the new leader, who became the founder of the dynasty of the Ṣaffārids. About the same time a similar dynasty, the Sāmānids, were establishing themselves in north-east Persia and Transoxiana.[2]

The new phenomenon thus consists in the appearance of leaders who have such military force at their command that they are virtually independent. The caliph is not strong enough to make them obey him. Some may originally have been provincial governors, others the leaders of a rising. Yet all are recognized by the caliphs as governors of the territories they actually rule, and members of their family who succeed to their power are similarly recognized. In this way there originated many dynasties of these *de facto* rulers. Occidental historians of the Islamic world often refer to them as 'sultans', but the Arabic word *sulṭān* ('authority') is used more widely and at times was applied to the caliph. The term 'war-lord' is therefore used here as both descriptive and distinctive. The war-lords were men who came to rule through their military power, but who did not claim to rule in their own right. Though the caliph was powerless against them, they were content to be in theory his subordinates. Perhaps they felt that this strengthened them by giving their rule an appearance of legitimacy.

The military power of the ʿAbbāsids decreased throughout the ninth century. Instead of civilian levies they began to employ professionals–especially Turkish mercenaries–who were militarily effective, but whose presence led to an imbalance at the centre of the empire. Things went from bad to worse. In 936 the caliph tried the experiment of giving supreme power–and the title of 'grand emir' or 'emir of emirs' (*amīr al-umarā'*)–to an administrator who controlled some military force. The experiment was unsuccessful, however. In 945 Baghdad was forcibly entered by the armies of a family of war-lords, the Būyid or Buwayhid dynasty.[3] They were duly 'appointed' by the caliphs, but their appointment was not to a distant province but to the central lands of the empire. From this time onwards the ʿAbbāsid caliphs had no political power though they retained many ceremonial duties. The extent of territory under the war-lords ruling Baghdad varied from time to time according to their strength. In the eleventh century the Būyids declined, and in 1055 Baghdad fell into the hands of the Seljūqs. After more than a century they also were replaced at the centre. Finally in the middle of the thirteenth century came the Mongol invasion, the sack of Baghdad in 1258, and the extinction of the ʿAbbāsid caliphate of Baghdad.

The theory underlying the position of the war-lords was that they were persons 'appointed' by the caliph to military and administrative functions. Apart from this there was no religious basis for their rule. The Būyids were Shīʿites, and with their support the moderate or Twelver Shīʿites became better organized and elaborated a legal rite or system which was given recognition along with the four great Sunnite rites. The Seljūqs, on the other hand, were Sunnites and, as already mentioned, deliberately used Sunnism and especially Ashʿarite theology to strengthen and consolidate their power.

Apart from the general conception of the position of war-lord in subordination to the caliph, the chief matters of interest from the standpoint of political theory are the various experiments to discover a satisfactory principle of succession. The Arabs had no law of primogeniture and only insisted that the succession should be within a certain family. Some of the war-lords from central Asia originally possessed a family structure with sufficient cohesion to hold together without undue difficulty for two or three generations. In some cases the Seljūq practice of appointing a 'tutor-guardian' (*atabeg*) for princes given a provincial command seems to have worked well, for these were older men, army commanders of slave origin, and in the best cases were devoted to the young princes; in other cases, however, they were mainly concerned with increasing their own power. The most interesting experiment was that of the slave-household, developed out of traditional Turkish forms; as a rule of succession it reached its climax in the Burjī Mamlūks who ruled Egypt from 1382 to 1517; but it also played an important part in the administrative structure of the Ottoman empire.[4]

2. The political theorists

It was stated in the Introduction that this book would be concerned with practice more than theory, since 'in the Islamic world the concepts implicit in men's practice are more important than the writings of the political theorists'. An attempt must now be made to justify and elucidate this assertion, and to show the relation of the theory to the practice.

A convenient starting-point is the commonly held view among occidental students that 'The Ordinances of Government' (*Al-aḥkām as-sulṭāniyya*) by al-Māwardī (d. 1058) is the 'standard' account of the political thought of Islam. This view was questioned by Sir Hamilton Gibb, who, from the fact that the book was commissioned by one of the ʿAbbāsid caliphs and from points in its treatment, argued that it must have contemporary relevance.[5] In particular it is defending the position of the caliph against the Būyid war-lords who were ruling in Baghdad, and against the Fāṭimids ruling in Cairo, who now claimed to be the rightful rulers of the whole Islamic world. It likewise showed how the caliph's claim could be upheld despite the dominance of the Būyids, and how his relationship to Sunnite war-lords (like Maḥmūd of Ghazna) was to be conceived. The general conclusion is that Sunnite political theory is not a blue-print for the future, but rather a form of reflection on the history of the Islamic community up to this point–'the *post eventum* justification of the precedents which have been ratified by ijmāʿ'.[6]

The relationship of Sunnite political theory to the practice of the community was further considered by the same writer in an article entitled 'Some Considerations on the Sunni Theory of the Caliphate'.[7] He sees the caliphate as 'the symbol of the supremacy of the Sharīʿa' and as 'that form of government which safeguards the ordinances of the Sharīʿa and sees that they are put into practice'.[8] He feels, however, that al-Māwardī began to move along 'the path of compromise', and that under subsequent writers this path brought Sunnite (or at least Ashʿarite) political theory to collapse. By this he appears to mean that theory failed to make any credible assertion about a particular person having a *right* to rule, and in the end regarded rule seized by force as legitimate.

Reflection on these 'considerations' prompts the reader to ask whether such writers as al-Māwardī were aiming at constructing a political theory of what rule was legitimate. When the ʿAbbāsid government about the middle of the ninth century decided that it must placate the ulema and their following among the masses, it did not completely surrender to their point of view. In effect the ulema were allowed to control the social fabric, but they were given virtually no voice in the other aspects of government, and indeed they had paid little attention to these aspects and had little to say about them. What the ulema were above all concerned to maintain was the charismatic or divinely-instituted nature of the community, and of this they saw the guarantee in its possession—not its carrying out in full—of the divinely-given law, the Sharīʿa.

If one were starting *de novo* to frame a constitution to ensure the supremacy of the Sharīʿa, there are various ways in which it would seem possible to do this. The corps of ulema might have been regarded as an independent body whose function was to maintain the supremacy of the Sharīʿa. Another course which would have seemed possible would have been to regard the war-lord, where he was prepared to listen to the ulema in the spheres of chief concern to them, as himself the guarantor of the Sharīʿa. The first of these possibilities was doubtless rejected because the judicature became the main career-opening of the ulema, and the judges belonged to the executive function and as such were subordinate to the chief executive officer, the caliph. Something like the second course was in fact adopted by Ibn-Khaldūn and the Persian Jalāl-ad-Dīn Dawānī (often called ad-Dawwānī) in the fifteenth century. In the second half of the tenth century, however, apart from the fact that various war-lords had acknowledged the nominal suzerainty of the caliph, it would have been difficult to regard the Buwayhid war-lords as guarantors of the Sharīʿa because of their Shīʿite views. In this way the type of theory of which al-Māwardī is the best representative became current, and remained in vogue for several centuries.

It will be convenient at this point to quote what Sir Hamilton Gibb says in concluding his review of Sunnite political thought:

> As is so often the case in Islam, the inner reality is quite other than would appear from the external formulations of the jurists. Between the real content of Muslim thought and its juristic expression there is a certain dislocation, so that it is seldom possible to infer the reality from the outer form. Only when both are known can the relation between them be discerned; and the formula is then seen to be an attempt, not so much to express the inner principle as it is, as to compress it within a rigid mould in order to serve a legal argument and a partial end. But at the same time our survey furnishes an equally striking example of the converse truth, that Muslim thought refuses to be bound by

> the outward formulae. It exerts a constant pressure, whose influence is to be seen in that unobtrusive reshaping of theory which, beneath an outward inflexibility, characterizes all branches of speculative activity in Islam, where Islam has remained a living organism. And, if necessary, it does not hesitate to overstep the limits of theory and to give independent expression to its sense of realities.[8]

No work on Islamic political theory has adequately dealt with the problem thus adumbrated by Sir Hamilton Gibb, namely, that of the relationship of political theory to the historical realities. The fullest treatment so far written in English of Islamic political thought[9] unfortunately places it in a completely different context and sees it as reaching its highest point in the writings of al-Fārābī, Avicenna (Ibn-Sīnā) and Averroes (Ibn-Rushd). These men were, of course, outstanding in metaphysics and other branches of philosophy, and their political writings, as part of their general philosophy, reached a high level of technical competence. But if, as is suggested, 'it was the study of Platonic philosophy which gave their own philosophy its character and its form',[10] sometimes modified by the ideas of Aristotle and later commentators, then we shall not expect these writers to be the best guides to the distinctive aspects of Islamic political thought. There is indeed much that is distinctively Islamic in them, but they had less influence even than the jurists on the main body of Sunnite Islam.

In the history of political theory in Islam there is thus a wide and virtually uncultivated field to which it is to be hoped some young scholars will ere long devote themselves. It is a difficult field, for the theorists must be looked at in their historical context, and the student must also be aware of the points on which debate concentrated at any given time. In the course of such a study more will perhaps be learnt about Islam in general than about its effective political concepts.

APPENDED NOTE

A preliminary list of political theorists

The following is a list of the chief works or types of work to be considered in a history of Islamic political theory. This list is in no way complete, but is composed mainly of works that are easily accessible or which are of *prima facie* importance. Works in the Persian tradition are also relevant but are not included here since they have been mentioned above (pp. 81-2).

(1) Abū-Yūsuf (d. 798), a pupil of Abū-Ḥanīfa who did much to establish the Ḥanafite legal rite, wrote a book on the land-tax (*kharāj*) for Hārūn ar-Rashīd.[11] This is available in a French translation as *Le livre de l'impôt foncier*, by E. Fagnan (Paris, 1921). The introductory remarks occupy some twenty pages and deal with the duties of princes and their relations to their subjects. This is interesting for its early date.

(2) It became customary to have a section on the 'imamate' in most treatises on theology. Al-Ashʿarī (d. 935), the founder of the Ashʿarite theological school, has short chapters in various works, notably at the end of *Kitāb al-Lumaʿ*. This is translated by R. J. McCarthy in *The Theology of al-Ashʿarī* (Beirut, 1953) 112-16.[12]

(3) The Ashʿarite school is often contrasted with the Māturīdite, though the parallelism is perhaps less than has been assumed. Sir Hamilton Gibb assigns to the Māturīdites an important influence on some later developments.[13] Al-Māturīdī (d. 944) and his followers were closely associated with the Ḥanafite legal rite. Early forms of the Ḥanafite creed are translated by A. J. Wensinck in *The Muslim Creed*.[14] The later views on the imamate are to be found in the creed of Najm-ad-Dīn an-Nasafī (d. 1142).[15]

(4) The important philosopher al-Fārābī (d. 950) wrote several works on politics of which the most important is that usually known by the shortened title of 'The Virtuous City' (*Al-madīna al-fāḍila*) or, as in the German translation of F. Dieterici, 'Der Musterstaat'.[16] Readily available in English is the translation by D. M. Dunlop of 'Aphorisms of the Statesman' (*Fuṣūl al-Madanī*).[17] Since al-Fārābī spent the last years of his life at the court of the Shīʿite (Ḥamdānid) ruler of Aleppo, it has been asked whether he was a Shīʿite; while there are some indications that his outlook was not wholly Shīʿite, much of his thought would fit in well with Shīʿite conceptions.[18]

(5) The chief work of the Fāṭimid form of Ismāʿīlite

Shīʿism is 'The Pillars of Islam' (*Daʿāʾim al-islām*) by the Qāḍī an-Nuʿmān (d. 974).[19]

(6) An early Imāmite Shīʿite creed with a section on politics is that of ash-Shaykh aṣ-Ṣadūq al-Qummī (d. 991), translated into English by A. A. A. Fyzee.[20]

(7) Ashʿarite views were developed by several thinkers during the eleventh century. Al-Bāqillānī (d. 1013) has included a long section on the imamate in his general work on theology known as the *Tamhīd* or 'Introduction'.[21]

(8) In Avicenna (Ibn-Sīnā) (d. 1037) Neoplatonic philosophy in Arabic may be said to reach its climax. He had played a part in politics in various minor courts east of Baghdad, even rising to be vizier for a time. At this period the Fāṭimids were felt to be a menace, and it is not surprising that the discussions of political theory in various works of Avicenna show him to be closer to Sunnism than was al-Fārābī.[22]

(9) Another eleventh-century Ashʿarite is al-Baghdādī (d. 1037), who devoted a chapter of his general theological work, 'The Principles of Religion' (*Uṣūl ad-dīn*), to the imamate.[23]

(10) Al-Māwardī (d. 1058), whose 'Ordinances of Government' has already been mentioned above, was another Ashʿarite.[24]

(11) About the same time another work on 'The Ordinances of Government' was produced by the Ḥanbalite writer Abū-Yaʿlā ibn-al-Farrāʾ (d. 1065).[25]

(12) Another important Ashʿarite, al-Juwaynī, known as Imām al-Ḥaramayn (d. 1085) not merely had a chapter about the imamate in his general work on theology, *Al-irshād*, but devoted a special work to the subject, *Ghiyāth al-imām*, dedicated to the vizier Niẓām-al-Mulk.[26]

(13) Al-Juwaynī's famous pupil al-Ghazālī (d. 1111), besides discussing the imamate in theological works, wrote a defence of the caliphate against Fāṭimid claims. This latter work was written at the request of the ʿAbbāsid caliph al-Mustaẓhir and is known either as *Al-Mustaẓhirī* or as *Faḍāʾiḥ al-Bāṭiniyya*.[27]

(14) Completely different is the Third Discourse of *The Nasirean Ethics* of Naṣīr-ad-Dīn Ṭūsī (d. 1274). The writer was a Shīʿite who witnessed the transference of power from the

Ismāʿīlites of Alamut to the Mongols. He incorporates the Greek and Farabian conception of the Virtuous City.[28]

(15) A statement of the later form of the Imāmite Shīʿite doctrine of the imamate is found in a work (which has been translated into English) of the scholar known as ʿAllāma-i-Ḥillī (d. 1325).[29]

(16) Perhaps the most influential writer of this period is the great Ḥanbalite Ibn-Taymiyya (d. 1328). A careful study of his political theories has been made by Henri Laoust in his *Essai sur les doctrines sociales et politiques de Taḳī-d-Dīn Aḥmad b. Taimīya.*[30] Ibn-Taymiyya was a voluminous writer. The two chief works relevant to political theory are *Minhāj as-sunna an-nabawiyya* and *As-siyāsa ash-sharʿiyya*, of which the latter has been translated into French.[31]

(17) Badr-ad-Dīn ibn-Jamāʿa (d. 1333), a Shāfiʿite, lived like Ibn-Taymiyya in Egypt and Syria, and like him may be said to be adapting Sunnite theory to the situation created by the destruction of the ʿAbbāsid caliphate of Baghdad in 1258. His important work on political theory has been edited and translated into German.[32]

(18) Ibn-Khaldūn (d. 1406) was a statesman and historian who has been hailed as one of the first to attempt a scientific study of the state and society. This he did in his *Muqaddima* (or 'Introduction') to a large general history. There is an excellent English translation.[33]

(19) Western scholars have paid some attention–perhaps more than it merits–to the work of an Imāmite Shīʿite writer Jalāl-ad-Dīn ad-Dawānī (d. 1502), especially his *Akhlāq-i Jalālī*, translated into English as *The Practical Philosophy of the Muhammedan People.*[34] It is in the same tradition as *The Nasirean Ethics* (no. 14 above).

After these works there appears to be little of importance in political theory until the nineteenth century, by which time European influences were strong in the Islamic world.

3. The caliphate after 1258

The capture of Baghdad by the Mongols under Hulagu in 1258 is usually reckoned a turning-point in Islamic history. We are not here concerned with the general effects of the Mongol invasion and its savage massacres of city-dwellers and other inhabitants of the various lands. Rather as a side-effect the invasion brought to an end the ʿAbbāsid caliphate of Baghdad. Following on the capture of the city the reigning caliph was put to death. One of his brothers, with some nominal support from Egypt, attempted to recover Baghdad, but was killed; and that was virtually the end. Latterly the ʿAbbāsids of Baghdad had had so little real influence in politics that their disappearance led to no appreciable change in practice, though it created a problem for the theorists. The title 'caliph' had come to be used by several rulers, so that the unique character of *the* caliphate had been obscured and forgotten. The influence of the theorists was slight and the great majority of practical administrators saw no point in restoring the office of caliph.

One ruler, however, seems to have thought that recognition by an ʿAbbāsid caliph would legitimize and strengthen his rule. This was the Mamlūk sultan of Egypt, Baybars, who installed a junior member of the ʿAbbāsid family as caliph in Cairo. This line of Cairene caliphs had even less power than their predecessors in Baghdad, since they were seldom recognized outside the Mamlūk dominions. They continued, however, until the Ottoman conquest of Egypt in 1517. The caliph at this date, al-Mutawakkil III, was taken to Istanbul by the conqueror, remained there for a time, and then returned to Cairo, where he died in 1543. He had apparently no successor as caliph. At a much later time, however–probably not until after 1750–Ottoman sultans claimed that al-Mutawakkil had transferred the caliphate to them. It is now held by modern historians, however, that this transfer was a fiction, intended to justify the sultans' claim to have a right of spiritual protection of all Muslims, comparable to that exercised by the Pope over Catholic Christians and by the Tsar of Russia over Orthodox Christians. The grounds for considering the transfer a fiction are that in contemporary documents where one might expect the title to appear it does not occur, whereas it was used in an unofficial and adulatory way of the sultans even before 1517. The truth is that in the early sixteenth century there was little interest in the title of 'caliph', and it was not felt to confer any great dignity.[35]

Once the caliphate had been resurrected in the eighteenth

century, however, it gained some recognition from Muslims throughout the world. Much of this was doubtless due to the fact that the Ottoman sultan had become by far the most powerful Muslim sovereign. The extent of the recognition gained is measured by the perturbation felt by Muslims all over the world when the Ottoman caliphate was finally abolished in 1924. This came about through the action of the Turkish Republic led by Mustafa Kemal Atatürk. In 1922 the last sultan was deposed and the sultanate abolished, but another member of the Ottoman family was appointed caliph with purely spiritual powers. This arrangement was only temporary, however, and in 1924 the caliphate was finally abolished. For a time Muslims in many parts of the world tried to find a way of continuing the caliphate, but no leader commanded universal approval, and the Caliphate Congress which met at Cairo and Mecca in 1926 decided in effect that the office must remain in abeyance for the visible future. It is conceivable that at some later date there may be a new caliphate, and this could have a strong emotional appeal. For the moment, however, the concept of the office of caliph has no practical relevance. Rule in Islamic countries is justified in other ways.

TEN

THE DEVELOPMENT OF SHĪʿITE ISLAM

1. 'Moderate' Shīʿism and the Imāmite party

Something has already been said about the manifestations of Shīʿism in the Umayyad and early ʿAbbāsid periods (ch. 3, § 4; 7, § 2). Fundamental to the appearance of Shīʿism was the belief–vague at the intellectual level, but held with vehemence –that security and prosperity were to be attained by following and obeying a leader with the charisma of 'the family', whether this was interpreted as the clan of Hāshim or as the descendants of 'Alī and Fāṭima or in some other way. From early in the eighth century and perhaps even earlier a specific man was recognized as head of the 'Alid group, but this position seems to have been without political significance and indeed little more than a family appointment. Jaʿfar aṣ-Ṣādiq (d. 765), the family leader when the ʿAbbāsids came to power, may for a time have toyed with the idea of a bid for the caliphate, but he soon realized that the ʿAbbāsids were too strong. For another century the family leaders–later called 'imams'–lived peaceably under ʿAbbāsid rule. The 'moderate' Shīʿites of this period, it has been asserted above, were not thinking of overthrowing ʿAbbāsid rule, but rather of making the government of the empire more autocratic. This group, mostly known as Rāfiḍites (Rawāfiḍ) by contemporaries, received a setback when, just before 850, the ʿAbbāsid government decided to rely mainly on the support of the constitutionalist bloc.

The crisis came in 874 or, more probably, a few years after that. In 874 one of the family leaders of the ʿAlids died, and about the same time his young son, the obvious successor, either died or otherwise disappeared. The conjectural reconstruction of events by a modern occidental writer would be that a few years after 874 one of the non-ʿAlid leaders among the 'moderate' Shīʿites saw that there was a great political advantage in reviving the idea of the 'hidden imam', and applying it to the young boy who had disappeared. The actual ʿAlid family leaders had shown little political competence, whereas a non-ʿAlid with political ability could proceed satisfactorily as agent of the 'hidden imam'. In this way he could reorganize the 'moderate' Shīʿites now that the ʿAbbāsid government was committed to supporting the Sunnites. The new political doctrine is best known as Imāmism or Imāmite Shīʿism. It asserted the existence of a line of twelve imams, or rightful heads of the whole Muslim community. The first three of these were ʿAlī and his sons al-Ḥasan and al-Ḥusayn, the sixth Jaʿfar aṣ-Ṣādiq, the eleventh the man who died in 874 (beginning of January), and the twelfth his son who had disappeared and was now 'hidden'. At an appropriate time he would return as the Mahdī, the man 'guided' by God who would set all things right. Because they thus recognized twelve imams they are also known as the Ithnāʿashariyya or Twelvers (in distinction from the Ismāʿīlīs who are Seveners–as will be explained in the next section).[1]

The proclamation of the new Imāmite ideas involved a rewriting of earlier history, which makes it difficult to know precisely what happened. According to the view suggested above, however, the political and intellectual activity out of which the Imāmite sect grew took place in the years just before and after 900. The names are known of several men who took part in this activity, but it is impossible to isolate the special contribution of each.[2] What is certain is that when the Būyid war-lords gained control of Baghdad in 945, they gave the fullest support to the Imāmite jurists, so that the Imāmites or Ithnāʿasharites came to be recognized as having a legal rite comparable to the main Sunnite ones. This is sometimes called the Jaʿfarī rite since they used many Traditions transmitted by Jaʿfar aṣ-Ṣādiq.

From the political angle the most important subsequent development of Imāmite Shīʿism was when in 1502 it became the official religion of the new Persian state being established by Shāh Ismāʿīl.[3] The latter, whose reign may be dated from 1501 to 1524, claimed to be a descendant of one of the twelve imams, and was acknowledged head of a mystical (dervish) order, whose members were also fighting men. This combination of the monk and the warrior appears bizarre to the occidental, but it has been frequently found in the Islamic world. The precise religio-political position of the Shāh of Persia under the Ṣafavids and later dynasties has not been adequately studied. Sometimes he was popularly regarded as divine or semi-divine and a reincarnation of one of the twelve imams. At other times he is spoken of rather as the agent of the hidden imam. Despite this position of theoretical autocracy the class of jurist-intellectuals, known as *mujtahids*, came to have a measure of power. It is not yet clear, however, how important these old concepts will be during the next half century. The decision about Shīʿism in 1502 certainly had the effect of isolating Persia from her neighbours while giving her greater internal religious homogeneity; and this provided a good basis for the development of nationalism in the nineteenth century.[4]

2. Revolutionary or 'Sevener' Shīʿism

If there is some obscurity about the organization of Imāmite Shīʿism in the period after 874, there is even greater obscurity about the beginnings of the other main form of Shīʿism, which may be labelled 'Sevener' (Sabʿiyya) though it has a great variety of names and subdivisions. The external and obvious difference between the Seveners and the Twelvers is that the Seveners hold that the sixth imam, Jaʿfar aṣ-Ṣādiq, was succeeded by a son Ismāʿīl, whereas the Twelvers hold that the imamate passed to another son, Mūsā al-Kāẓim, and then to his descendants down to the twelfth imam who disappeared. How exactly this division occurred cannot be stated with certainty, since the original events became the subject of vehement assertions and counter-assertions. It is probable that Ismāʿīl was the centre of some revolutionary plotting before the death of his father in 765, and that this revolutionary movement continued underground. What is definitely known is that at two points political power was seized by persons who were in some sense followers of Ismāʿīl. These were the Carmathians or Qarāmiṭa who gained power in Bahrein (Baḥrayn) about 894, and the Fāṭimids who established a small state in Tunisia in 909 and then conquered Egypt in 969.[5] The Fāṭimid state continued until 1171, but that of the Carmathians in Bahrein, though it lasted until about 1100, was ruled by a council of elders after 977.

In respect of political theory chief interest is in the concept of the imam. The imam is conceived as an autocratic ruler, and the actual Fāṭimid government was heavily centralized. The imam owed nothing to election by the people, but was given the imamate by the 'designation' (*naṣṣ*) of his predecessor, and may thus be said to have had a kind of 'divine right'. Moreover this was a right to rule over all Muslims. It was considered possible and indeed often normal that the imam should be 'hidden'; but in later days at least it was claimed that he was not completely hidden but was in contact with his authorized agent. At times this authorized agent was known as an acting or trustee imam (*imām mustawdaʿ*) as distinct from the true imam (*imām mustaqarr*).[6] Apparently the former sometimes became the adopted son of the true imam of the day, and in this capacity might be guardian of the imam designate who was normally a son of the true imam. The various shifts of the theory are, of course, so many attempts to bring it into line with the facts of history.

Because the Fāṭimids claimed that their imam was the rightful imam of all Muslims, they sent emissaries throughout the ʿAbbāsid domains propagating their religio-political views and seeking to gain supporters. Discontented elements in various areas accepted their doctrines. Their chief outward success was during the interregnum after the loss of power by the Būyids before the Seljūqs asserted their control of Baghdad. A general who actually ruled Baghdad for about a year professed to do so in the name of the Fāṭimid imam. After 1055, however, the Seljūqs were clearly too strong for a pro-Fāṭimid rising to have any prospect of success, and Fāṭimid propaganda slackened. Discontent continued, however, among those groups in Syria and Persia who had embraced Ismāʿīlite (Fāṭimid) doctrines. About the end of the eleventh century these groups decided to 'go it alone' without waiting for the Fāṭimid government in Cairo, and the manner in which they asserted their independence is worthy of being described.

The leader of the Ismāʿīlite movement in the ʿAbbāsid domains was al-Ḥasan ibn-aṣ-Ṣabbāḥ. He visited Egypt in 1078 and presumably realized Fāṭimid unwillingness or inability to give any effective support to his own movement. In 1090 he set the revolt on foot by capturing the remote fortress of Alamut. In 1094 the Fāṭimid caliph al-Mustanṣir died after a long reign, and court intrigue led to the disappearance of his son and designated heir Nizār and the elevation to the throne of another son al-Mustaʿlī. Al-Ḥasan adroitly maintained that his allegiance was given to Nizār, and in this way became effective head of the eastern Ismāʿīlites without making the impossible claim that he himself belonged to the family of the Prophet. He claimed to be in touch with Nizār, but at some point he must surely have realized that he had lost all contact with him.[7]

The subsequent history of the Ismāʿīlites is a fascinating example of how the political implications of a religious doctrine may be completely transformed. During the revolt which began in 1090 the Nizārian Ismāʿīlites, nicknamed 'hashish-men' or in a Europeanized form 'Assassins', made a practice of political assassination (and thereby gave their name to this activity). Groups of both Nizārians and Mustaʿlians made their way to India, and there were further schisms in each camp. The majority of the Mustaʿlians in India are today known as Bohorās. Some of the Nizārians there are known as Khojas; but the best known and most important group of Nizārians are the followers of the Agha Khan, who are widely scattered in many countries, but are specially strong in East Africa. From being a body of assassins and revolutionaries they have become a prosperous closely-knit community of business men with well-organized welfare services for their less fortunate fellow-members.[8]

3. Zaydite Shīʿism

For the sake of completeness some reference should be made to Zaydite Shīʿism. The name is derived from Zayd, son of the fourth imam, ʿAlī Zayn-al-ʿĀbidīn, and grandson of the Ḥusayn who died at Kerbela. Zayd died in an unsuccessful rising against the Umayyads in 740. Various groups attached themselves to his name during the early ʿAbbāsid period and later, though their connection with his immediate followers is not clear. Their distinctive point of theory is that before any member of 'the family' can be accepted as imam he must claim the title publicly and back up his claim by force. In other words they reject the doctrine of the 'hidden imam'. Some of them held theological views close to those of the sect of Muʿtazilites.

Small states based on Zaydite theories were founded about the middle of the ninth century, one in Daylam on the southern shores of the Caspian Sea, and another in the Yemen. The former disappeared about the twelfth century, but the latter, with some interruptions, has continued to exist until the present day.[9]

The Zaydites may be said to represent a compromise between Sunnism and the more thorough-going Shīʿite views with their main emphasis on the imam or charismatic leader. The roots of the political thinking which controls the activity of contemporary Muslims are to be found in Sunnism; but Shīʿism shows the deep desire and indeed yearning of many Muslims for a divinely guided leader.

ELEVEN

EPILOGUE: ISLAM IN CONTEMPORARY POLITICS

1. Islam and occidental political ideas

Political writing under the influence of occidental ideas began among Muslims in the nineteenth century, and grew to a flood in the twentieth. It is not proposed here to review this material in detail, but merely to offer some general reflections.[1]

It is obvious that at different times and places European ideas have been enthusiastically accepted by particular groups. It is not so obvious that, despite the enthusiasm, this acceptance has been only partial and limited. Often a show was made of taking over European institutions in order to impress on European statesmen that Islamic countries were rapidly transforming themselves into 'modern' states. This was especially so with the Ottoman empire in the nineteenth century. Frequently this led to a slavish imitation of details without much appreciation of the reasons for a practice. The Egyptian Parliament under the monarchy produced a record of its proceedings comparable to Hansard, though in the circumstances of Egyptian politics it is unlikely that the use made of the copy was a tenth of that made of the original. It is reported that in the 1950s the Chaplain of the House of Commons received a letter from a gentleman in a new Muslim state saying he had been appointed as Chaplain to his parliament and asking what were the duties of such an office. Other motives also have made European political ideas acceptable. Sometimes, for example, a concept has tended to promote the interests of a particular class.

(a) *Nationalism.* An idea that appears to have been widely accepted in Islamic countries is that of nationalism. This idea has been specially useful in the struggle against the colonialism and imperialism of the occidental powers. The right of 'national self-determination' was one to which it was in theory difficult for these powers to object. Thus nationalism was prominent during the struggle for independence, especially among those sections of the population with some higher education on the European model. It perhaps also became partly identified with the endemic xenophobia of the lower classes. Once independence was attained, however, nationalism gave little guidance for the subsequent development of the state.

The detailed application of the concept of nationalism was full of difficulty. The simplest case was that of Iran or Persia, where, as explained above, a foundation for nationalism had been created by the adoption of Imāmite Shīʿism as the official religion at the beginning of the sixteenth century. For a time the governing class of the Ottoman empire tried to proceed on the basis of a hypothetical Ottoman nationalism; but this concept met with little response, and the rival concept of Turkish nationalism proved stronger and contributed to the formation of the Turkish Republic. The Turkish leaders, however, were careful not to allow their nationalism to extend to Turkish peoples in Central Asia, for that would have looked like expansionism and might have led to international complications.

Arab nationalism is a complex subject, but is worthy of somewhat fuller treatment. A Christian Arab, George Antonius, in his book *The Arab Awakening*, first published in 1938, claimed that the national movement began in Beirut in a secret society about 1875. While there was some heightening of national self-awareness about this time, it is now usually held that there was no movement of political significance until the turn of the century. The clearest statements of belief from the Arabs as a nation are found in the writings of a Syrian called al-Kawākibī, published in Egypt between 1898 and his death in 1902. The traditional view tended to be that an Arab was such by descent–that is, he was a man whose ancestors had once been nomads in Arabia. In 1915 in the negotiations before the entry of the Arabs into the First World War the Sharīf of Mecca, acting as a spokesman for 'the whole of the Arab nation', was content to name the Red Sea as the western border of Arab territories. This implied that the Egyptians, though speaking Arabic, were not Arabs; and indeed few of them could claim Arab descent. For a time many Egyptians had no desire to call themselves Arabs, and instead tried to develop a separate Egyptian nationalism which looked back to the common Pharaonic heritage; Egypt had often been marked off from the rest of the Islamic world, and since 1805 had been largely independent. There were comparable attempts to develop a local nationalism in several of the states into which the Arab world had come to be divided, notably Syria and Iraq. The Arabs of the Arabian peninsula were less westernized and still conscious rather of descent. In the French-ruled territories, again, the intellectual élite had received a French education and were slow to develop a specific Arab consciousness.

A new conception of what an Arab is was developing in the period between the wars. By 1938, when Arab students in Europe held a conference in Brussels, it was possible to define as Arabs 'all who are Arab in their language, culture and loyalty', the latter term being taken to connote 'national feeling'.[2] This was, of course, more in line with European thinking and produced, potentially, a much larger nation. It was also more realistic. Descent was often difficult to prove. By the criterion of descent many Muslims from the Indian sub-continent and south-east Asia might have claimed to be Arabs, and many town-dwellers in Syria and Iraq might have difficulty in establishing their claims. Language is a more satisfactory criterion, but in 1938 there were still many Arabic-speaking Jews in various Arab countries, while Maltese could be regarded as a dialect of Arabic. The criterion of culture excludes the Maltese people, who would hate to be considered Arab, while their contention that Maltese should now be reckoned a distinct language from Arabic is generally accepted. The Arabic-speaking Jews to a great extent shared the culture of their Muslim neighbours. Many, including all those with Zionist views, have gone to Israel. Of those who are left some go so far in certain contexts as to speak of themselves as 'Arabs'. In difficult cases of this kind the criterion of 'loyalty' or 'national feeling' may be applied to the individual.

The new concept of what an Arab is, led to a realization among Arab statesmen, notably Gamal Abd-an-Nasser of Egypt, that pan-Arabism now had great potentialities. The same concept was also implicit in the Arab League, since membership of this body was open to all 'independent Arab states'. The founding members in 1945 were: Syria, Trans-Jordan, Iraq, Sa'udi Arabia, Lebanon, Egypt and the Yemen. The presence of Egypt showed the influence of the new concept of Arab. The influence of the concept was strengthened during the next two decades through the struggle of various countries to gain independence. This can be seen from the additions to the membership of the League during these decades: Libya (1953), Sudan (1956), Morocco and Tunisia (1958), Kuwait (1961), Algeria (1962). According to the latest figures available at the end of 1966 the total population of the members of the League was 106 millions. While this included a number of Berbers, Kurds and non-Muslim Sudanese, there were Arabs outside the League in Israel, the coastal areas of Arabia from Aden to Bahrein, the states of Mauritania and Chad, and perhaps one or two other places in Africa. The new concept of Arab has thus found an important political embodiment.

The significance of these developments can be examined from different angles. Here the religious one – the relation of nationalism to Islam – will be given prominence. One point to be remembered is that there are two or three million Christian Arabs, and that some of these have been enthusiastic Arab nationalists, especially during the earlier phases of the Arabic literary renaissance. More and more, however, it seems to have been held that Islam is a necessary constituent of Arab nationalism; and several Christian Arabs have tended to accept this view.[3] The culture of most Christian Arabs is of course heavily islamized, and it is difficult for them to avoid regarding Muḥammad as a 'national' hero. Lecturing in Chicago in 1945 Sir Hamilton Gibb spoke of the dangers of nationalism for Islam and its lack of deep roots in the Muslim soul.[4] Yet as one reflects on all that has happened since then, one is bound to wonder whether Arab nationalism has not in part been transformed. For a time it may have been a useful stick with which to beat the Europeans. In the end, however, it looks as if it has become a partial political realization of Islamic solidarity.

This question of the relation of Islam and nationalism has many aspects. There is the nation of Pakistan, for example, in the case of which 'being a Muslim' was a constitutive element of nationhood, since Pakistan is formed out of the predominantly Muslim areas of the Indian sub-continent; yet even here there is a difference between being a Muslim and being a Pakistani. In contrast to Pakistan there is found in most parts of the Islamic world what might be called a secular Islamic nationalism. This describes the attitude of those men whose religious belief and practice is almost non-existent, but who feel a deep loyalty to Islamic society as a cultural entity. There is the student, for example, who openly denies the existence of God, but who will vehemently defend Islam if an occidental attacks it.

The point to which the various lines of thought here suggested all direct the observer is the profound reality of Islamic solidarity – the brotherhood of all Muslims. So far the attempts to find appropriate political concepts to express this solidarity have been inadequate. Some Muslims have dreamed of a pan-Islamic political unity, but others have objected to this in practice. In the visible future it is unlikely that all Muslims will be embraced in a single body politic. Despite this inability to find outward expression the solidarity is real. It is a reality of the kind on which men fall back when the tensions in which they live increase. It is thus in the longer perspective a factor to be taken seriously by statesmen even if its immediate relevance is slight.[5]

(b) *Democracy, totalitarianism, and socialism*. It might have been expected that many Arabs would have been ready to transform their polities into democracies.[6] There is a democratic element in the Arab tribe, and the assembly of all the tribesmen is not unlike the assembly of the citizens of a Greek *polis*. Experience has shown, however, that the democratic element in the Arab tribe is not a sufficient foundation for the institutions of representative government associated with modern democracies. Perhaps this insufficiency is due to the fact that the business of the tribe is conducted through the personal meeting of man with man. In a vast modern democracy there is much impersonality. Men are grouped with others in parties on the basis of a party programme or common policy. This is something, however, which the Arabs have found difficult. Contemporary Arab politics have much of the personal element. Where there are parties, they are usually based on personal allegiances, and not on an abstract and impersonal policy.

Again, if one thinks of democracy as government in the interests of the whole people, this does not fit in easily with Arab ideas. As has been noted above, Islam does not normally think of the rights of man because it is more conscious of the commands of God. The interests of ordinary people were usually well looked after in Islamic lands, but this came about through the labours of the ulema, and through the readiness of rulers to defer to the views of the ulema in many matters affecting ordinary people. Where the rulers were less attentive to the needs of ordinary man, there was little that could be done about it, for this was a point on which the Sharīʿa was weak. On the other hand, in so far as the great mass of the people approved of the Sharīʿa and had a deep allegiance to the Islamic community, of which the Sharīʿa was a constitutive element, government in accordance with the Sharīʿa might be said to proceed from 'the will of the people'.

The desire to have an Islamic constitution, as in Pakistan, Egypt and the Sudan, is in part the acceptance of a European idea, namely, that of constitutional government. The difficulties in framing an Islamic constitution for a modern state are formidable, since at many points the Islamic political tradition is far from being clear and unambiguous. It would seem, however, that it should be possible to produce a constitution in accordance with the central principles of the Sharīʿa. In so far as this is achieved, and the appropriate laws accepted and obeyed by both ruler and ruled, the state will approximate to a modern European democracy in the concern it shows for the welfare of the ordinary citizen.

Islamic polities are sometimes accused of being totalitarian, and thus anti-democratic. The accusation has an appearance of truth as regards the older Islamic world. The establishment controlled not only the administration but also the intellectual outlook of the masses. Heavy pressure was brought to bear on deviations, and most of them disappeared. Yet there was an important difference between the Islamic world and Hitler's Germany or Stalin's Russia. Hitler controlled the ideas of National-Socialism and Stalin was the chief official exponent of the ideas of Marx and Lenin. In the Islamic world, on the other hand, the men with actual political power never had control of ideas. The religious institution was part of the establishment, but it also maintained a degree of independence. In particular the theory was everywhere accepted among Sunnites that the most powerful sultan is subject to the Sharīʿa just like the humblest Muslim. If the sultan disobeys God's commands, he may escape punishment in this life, but will have to pay in the world to come. Thus no sultan or other ruler of Sunnite Muslims has anything like the power over men's thinking possessed by the occidental totalitarian dictator.

The strange interplay of traditional and modern forces is illustrated by a recent incident, in itself trivial. In December 1966 the Supreme Court of the Republic of the Sudan overruled a government decision which had the effect of making the Communist party unlawful in the Sudan; but the government refused to accept the decision of the Supreme Court and continued to treat the Communist party as unlawful. In this incident there is implicit, on the one hand, the traditional view that the judge, being appointed by the ruler, is subordinate to him and can be overruled by him. There is thus no support for the occidental idea of an independent judicature. Yet many of the benefits accruing in the West from the independence of the judicature were secured in Islamic countries by the dominance of the Sharīʿa. The difficulty at the present day is that there are many points at which the guidance of the Sharīʿa, as traditionally conceived, is inadequate. There is thus great urgency about the adaptation of the Sharīʿa to contemporary needs.

There is also much talk nowadays of 'Islamic socialism' just as there is of 'African socialism'. Both are usually contrasted with Marxist socialism. Especially in the case of African socialism, there is grave danger that this idea may be used by ruling groups to justify policies by which they advance their own interests at the expense of their opponents. In the case of Islamic socialism this is at least more difficult in theory, since the content of Islamic socialism must be linked with the Sharīʿa. In practice the difference may not be so great, since the Sharīʿa has not been elaborated in order to guide men in respect of the problems of the modern state. Yet the bare theoretical presence of the Sharīʿa, despite its inadequacies, may one day prevent the appearance of a totalitarianism on the Hitlerian model.

In general, then, it may be concluded that the adoption of occidental ideas by Muslims has usually served some pre-existing Islamic purposes and that the political life of Muslims is controlled by age-old patterns. Two matters are specially prominent: first, the real solidarity of the *umma* or community of all Muslims; and secondly, the existence of the Sharīʿa as a divinely given *sunna* or model of social life.

2. Actualizing possibilities of adaptation

Much water has run under the bridges since Lord Cromer wrote that 'Islam reformed is Islam no longer'.[7] Great changes have taken place in the lives of Muslims, and nevertheless—even if some observers might want to argue the point—it would generally be thought that Islam remains Islam. As one considers the continuing need of Islam to adapt itself to meet the problems of the contemporary world, it is unsatisfactory to speculate in the void about possibilities of adaptation. On the other hand, if one looks carefully at Islamic history, one will find many instances where adaptation has actually taken place; and the analysis of such instances will give us a clue to what may happen in the immediate future. All established religions tend to be conservative and to dislike change; but Islam is characterized by an extreme degree of resistance to change, and this gives some justification to Lord Cromer's remark. Part of the reason is the nomadic Arab's deep-seated belief that safety lies in keeping to the *sunna* or beaten path followed by the ancestors of the tribe. The same attitude is occasionally found in the Old Testament, as in the verse: 'Thus saith the Lord . . . ask for the old paths, where is the good way, and walk therein, and ye shall find rest for your souls'.[8] Despite the strength of this attitude in Islam adaptive changes have taken place in the past, and this justifies one in expecting that Islam will adapt itself to meet contemporary problems.

One of the ways in which an adaptive change occurs is through the appearance of a charismatic leader. Muḥammad himself was such a person. By his claim to the charisma of prophethood he was able to bring the Arabs to accept revolutionary changes in their lives. Once the changes had been effected there was a tendency for the conservative attitude to reassert itself, but now it was to preserve the new *sunna* or beaten path, the *sunna* of Muḥammad. In the subsequent centuries of Islamic history there are many instances of men coming forward as leaders on the basis of some charismatic gift, and through the movement thus inaugurated adapting Islam to the contemporary situation, at least at the local level. Although belief in the charismatic leader is a distinctive feature of the Shīʿites, many of the instances of successful adaptation have been in predominantly Sunnite regions. This has come about through a leader's claim to be the Mahdī or 'divinely guided one'. Expectation of the Mahdī among Muslims is roughly comparable to expectation of the Messiah among Jews.[9]

Among the men who have claimed this dignity or something similar three may be mentioned here: Ibn-Tūmart; Usuman dan-Fodio; and Muḥammad Aḥmad, the Mahdī of the Sudan. The movement of Ibn-Tūmart (d. 1130) led to the foundation of the empire of the Almohads (*al-muwaḥḥidūn*), who for nearly a century controlled all north-west Africa, and for half that period also ruled Islamic Spain. Usuman (ʿUthmān) dan-Fodio was a religious leader in West Africa who in 1804 declared a *jihād* or holy war against local rulers who claimed to be Muslims, but whose Islam he denied. Out of this war there developed the sultanate of Sokoto with its associated sultanates, sometimes known as the Fulani empire, and the basis of the Northern Nigeria of today. The movement had Mahdistic features and Usuman seems to have been regarded as the Mahdī in some quarters; though he explicitly denied that he was the Mahdī, he encouraged the Muslims of the region to expect the Mahdī in the near future.[10] The Mahdī of the Sudan formed an army and a state which for a dozen years (1885-98) the British were unable to master.[11]

In each of these instances it will be found that the leader was first and foremost a religious teacher. Young men were attracted by his teaching, and also some who were not so young. What he taught and preached was Islamic doctrine, but there were special emphases. These, if examined carefully, will be found to refer to the contemporary situation and to provide a focus and outlet for local discontent. Some of Ibn-Tūmart's distinctive doctrines, for example, were attacks on features of the rather similar movement in power in north-west Africa in his time (the Almoravids or *al-murābiṭūn*). In the case of the other two there was teaching relevant to the discontent arising from the dislocation of traditional society through contacts with Europeans. In all three instances the distinctive form of Islamic doctrine became the centre or focus of a new and greater political unity, and this may be regarded as a satisfactory response to the problems of the time.

Europeans have sometimes criticized both Mahdism and Islam generally for adopting a policy of propagating religious doctrines by military force.[12] This is to misunderstand the essentially religious character of the Mahdist movements. It is true, however, that the conception of the Mahdī and the holy war could be perverted to promote the ends of an individual or group. The holy war of which the Mahdī was leader was in some cases interpreted in stricter terms than in Muḥammad's time, and was then waged not only against pagans, but also against heretical Muslims; and the heresy could easily be stretched so that it included nearby tribes from which one could capture slaves for sale. Despite this possibility of perversion, however, the new emphases of the Mahdī or other leader were essentially attempts to adapt inherited religious doctrines to contemporary problems. From our present standpoint the interest of these historical instances is that they show how the charisma of a leader may generate sufficient enthusiasm among his followers to bring them to accept changes in religious teaching and practice, together with the consequent political and social changes.

A second way in which adaptive changes have come about is through the activities of the ulema or, more generally, the intellectuals. In the earlier history of Islam there are two important spheres in which adaptive changes were successfully carried through by the intellectuals: the creation of the Sharīʿa and Sunnism in the ninth century, and the assimilation of Greek thought between the ninth and twelfth centuries.

Something has already been said about the elaboration of the Sharīʿa together with the various repercussions of this process in the lives of Muslims.[13] An important part of the achievement was that the ideals and practices of nomadic society as modified by Muḥammad himself for life in the Medina of his day were further adapted to the more sophisticated cities of the Middle

East in the ninth century. This achievement was the outcome of a vast amount of intellectual activity. First there were the circles of pious men in the mosques of the chief cities who discussed the application of Islamic principles to contemporary questions. This was the beginning of a great work of systematization. After the coming to power of the ʿAbbāsids in 750 there was pressure on the various pious groups to move towards some degree of uniformity, and this meant further systematization. In the course of this further process it came to be generally accepted that approved practices should be justified by reference to the example of Muḥammad; and this example was witnessed to by Traditions. The setting up of criteria to distinguish sound from dubious Traditions, the collection of sound Traditions, and, on the basis of these, the working out of the details of a code of conduct for the increasing numbers of city-dwellers in the Islamic world – all this was achieved by the efforts of countless religious intellectuals. The change was brought about, too, without it becoming obvious that there had been a change, for the community still seemed simply to be following the example of Muḥammad. Certainly they were following him, but at the same time there had been adaptation; and the concealment of the adaptation perhaps made further adaptation more difficult.

The other way in which the intellectuals achieved adaptation was in the assimilation of Greek thought, including medicine and other sciences. The adaptation was necessary because Greek thought was the supreme intellectual achievement of Mediterranean and Middle Eastern man up to this point in time, and there was little contact with the Indian and Chinese traditions. Greek thought was the intellectual heritage of the educated men in Egypt, Syria and Iraq who from the eighth century onwards became converts to Islam; and such persons had necessarily to bring their new faith into harmony with their intellectual heritage. Many Muslims, too, including the caliphs, had a practical interest in Greek medicine and astronomy (the latter for its astrological aspect); and it was difficult to study these without also studying Greek philosophy. Apologists for Islam became aware of the strong arguments derived by their opponents from Greek philosophy and logic. Altogether there was wide interest in Greek thought, and this led to numerous translations of Greek works, some indirectly from the Syriac and others directly from the Greek.[14] The work of translation was first organized by al-Ma'mūn (caliph 813-33).

Translation, of course, was not itself the process of assimilation, though it was the basis for it. Some theologians began to adapt Greek arguments and ideas for apologetic purposes; and from this there followed bitter debates between Muslims who approved of such arguments and those who disapproved. There was always a tendency for those who approved of theological arguments in the Greek style to go too far in their acceptance of Greek ideas. This is generally held to have happened to the theological group known as the Mu'tazilites. The first stage in assimilation may be said to have been attained when the theologian al-Ash'arī (d. 935), though trained by the Mu'tazilites, decided to break with them and to use their type of argument in defence of the widely accepted Sunnite forms of Islamic doctrine. By this time there had appeared the so-called 'Philosophers' (Falāsifa)–men who claimed to be Muslims but who held views which were essentially Neoplatonist. The best known are al-Fārābī (d. 950) and Avicenna or Ibn-Sīnā (d. 1037), whose argumentation was technically superior to that of the contemporary Sunnite theologians. The second stage in assimilation occurred when the theologian al-Ghazālī (d. 1111) mastered the teaching of the Philosophers, employed its logical methods in his theology and indicated which of its metaphysical doctrines were incompatible with the Qur'ān and Sunnite teaching. From this time onwards most Islamic theologians accepted and used the technical aspects of Greek thought, while rejecting much Greek metaphysics. Islam had gained a place for itself in the highest reaches of the intellectual life of the time and region. This was a notable achievement of adaptation.

Yet a third way of bringing about a change to adapt Islamic teaching and practice to new circumstances is to be seen in *ijmā'* or 'consensus'–primarily the consensus of the whole community of Muslims. Consensus may be regarded as an aspect of the solidarity of the community, already emphasized, and clearly no change can be effective unless it is eventually approved by the majority of Muslims. Part of the achievement of the intellectuals in bringing about adaptations is that they gain the approval of the masses. Yet the consensus of the community does not always tamely follow the intellectuals. The case is frequently quoted of how the ulema declared the drinking of coffee forbidden but eventually had to permit it because the consensus of the people as a whole was strongly against them.[15] The consensus or common feeling of the Muslim community is thus a force to be reckoned with, even if it moves slowly.

These then are three ways in which in the past the Islamic community has in fact adapted itself to new situations. How far do they justify us in drawing conclusions about the future? In respect of the first and third ways nothing certain can be said. The appearance of a charismatic leader is always a possibility, but one cannot say beforehand where and when he is likely to appear. Even after he has appeared, one cannot tell whether his influence is going to be local and temporary or world-wide and lasting. Similarly the acceptance of change through the consensus of the community is often possible but seldom predictable beforehand. With regard to the second way, however–the activities of the intellectuals–a little may be said about the future, since there has already been some activity to meet the new situation. Roughly comparable to the original elaboration of the Sharīʿa are the attempts to bring Islamic social practices closer to European, especially in matters connected with the position of women. Here the ulema have achieved advances, while claiming not to change Islamic principles, or to revert to primitive Islamic practices which had been modified in the course of time. All this is reminiscent of what their predecessors did in the ninth century, but, while permitting many improvements, seems to rule out any radical readjustment to the contemporary world.

There are also developments at present which are comparable to the medieval assimilation of Greek thought, namely, the assimilation of European scientific thought. Here there are two groups of intellectuals: the ulema on the one hand, and those with a good European-type education on the other. Until now the two groups have had little contact with one another, just as the ulema of the eleventh and twelfth centuries had little contact with the Philosophers. Until recently the ulema had an education of the traditional type with no European admixture, while the modern intellectuals had received a minimum of instruction in the Islamic religion, and that at an elementary level. There are signs, however, that in due course the gulf between the two will be bridged. There has been some modernization of the courses at the Az'har university and at other centres; and some of the modern intellectuals are showing a growing interest in religion. Sir Mohammad Iqbal pioneered the way with his *Reconstruction of Religious Thought in Islam*,[16] where some influence of Bergson and Nietzsche is plain. Others are following, though none has yet attained the stature of Iqbal. Much further adaptation will undoubtedly take place, and in this way–who knows?–the scene may be set for the appearance of a charismatic leader who will become a world figure. If future developments take some such course, it is also likely that the Islamic world will remain faithful to its heritage, including its political heritage whose basic concepts have here been studied.

APPENDIX

THE CONSTITUTION OF MEDINA

(Ibn-Hishām, ed. Wüstenfeld, 341-3; Watt, *Medina*, 221-5)

In the name of God, the Merciful, the Compassionate.

This is a writing of Muḥammad the prophet between the believers and Muslims of Quraysh and Yathrib and those who follow them and are attached to them and who fight along with them.

1. They are a single community distinct from (other) people.
2. The Emigrants of Quraysh, according to their former approved practice, pay jointly the blood-money (incurred by one) among them, and ransom the captive of them, (doing this) with upright dealing and justice between the believers.
3. Banū ʿAwf, according to their former approved practice, pay jointly the previous blood-wits and each sub-group ransoms its captive, (doing this) with upright dealing and justice between the believers.
4. Banū l-Ḥārith, according to their former approved practice, pay jointly the previous blood-wits, and each subclan ransoms its captive(s), (doing so) with uprightness and justice between the believers.
5. Banū Sāʿida ... (as 3).
6. Banū Jusham ... (as 3).
7. Banū n-Najjār ... (as 3).
8. Banū ʿAmr b. ʿAwf ... (as 3).
9. Banū n-Nabīt ... (as 3).
10. Banū l-Aws ... (as 3).
11. The believers do not forsake a debtor among them, but give him (help), according to what is fair, for ransom or blood-wit.

12. A believer does not ally himself with the client of (another) believer without (the latter's) consent.
13. The God-fearing believers are against whoever of them acts wrongfully or seeks (? plans) an act that is unjust or treacherous or hostile or corrupt among the believers; their hands are all against him, even if he is the son of one of them.
14. A believer does not kill (another) believer (in vengeance) for an unbeliever, and does not 'help' an unbeliever against a believer.
15. The security (or protection) of God is one; the granting of 'neighbourly protection' by the least of (the believers) is binding on them (all); the believers are patrons (and clients) of one another to the exclusion of (other) people.
16. A Jew who follows us has (a right to) the same 'help' and support (as the believers), so long as they are not wronged (by him) and he does not 'help' (others) against them.
17. The peace of the believers is one; no believer makes peace (separately) apart from (other) believer(s), but (in any peace maintains) equality and fairness between them.
18. In every party that makes a razzia with us, one takes turns with another (at riding? at all military duties?).
19. The believers exact vengeance for one another where a man gives his blood in the way of God. The God-fearing believers are under the best and most correct guidance.
20. No idolater (among the clans of Medina?) gives 'neighbourly protection' for goods or person to (any of) Quraysh, nor intervenes on his behalf against a believer.
21. When anyone wrongfully kills a believer, the evidence being clear, then he is liable to be killed in retaliation for him, unless the representative of the victim is satisfied (with a payment). The believers are solidly against (the murderer), and may do nothing except oppose him.
22. A believer who has agreed to what is in this document and has believed in God and the Last Day may not 'help' or shelter a 'disturber'. Upon whoever 'helps' and shelters him is the curse and wrath of God on the day of

resurrection. Nothing will be accepted from him as compensation or restitution.

23. Wherever there is anything about which you differ, it is to be referred to God and to Muḥammad for a decision.
24. The Jews bear expenses along with the believers so long as they continue at war.
25. The Jews of Banū ʿAwf are a community along with the believers. To the Jews their religion and to the Muslims their religion. (This applies) both to their clients and to themselves, with the exception of anyone who has done wrong or acted treacherously; he brings evil only on himself and on his household.
26. For the Jews of Banū n-Najjār the like of what is for the Jews of Banū ʿAwf.
27. For the Jews of Banū l-Ḥārith the like . . .
28. For the Jews of Banū Sāʿida the like . . .
29. For the Jews of Banū Jusham the like . . .
30. For the Jews of Banū l-Aws the like . . .
31. For the Jews of Banū Thaʿlaba the like of what is for the Jews of Banū ʿAwf, with the exception of anyone who has done wrong or acted treacherously; he brings evil on himself and his household.
32. Jafna, a subdivision of Thaʿlaba, are like them.
33. For Banū sh-Shuṭayba the like of what is for the Jews of Banū ʿAwf; honourable dealing (comes) before treachery.
34. The clients of Thaʿlaba are like them.
35. The 'intimates' of (particular) Jews are as themselves.
36. None of (the believers) goes out (on a razzia) without the permission of Muḥammad, but a man is not prevented from avenging wounds. If a man kills (another unawares, or, more generally, acts rashly), (he involves only) himself and his household, except where he has been wronged. God is the truest (fulfiller) of this (document?).
37. It is for the Jews to bear their expenses and for the Muslims to bear their expenses. There is to be (mutual) 'help' between them against whoever wars against the people of this document. Between them there is to be (mutual) giving of advice, consultation, and honourable

dealing, not treachery. A man is not guilty of treachery through (the act of) his confederate. 'Help' is (to be given) to him who is wronged.

38. The Jews bear expenses along with the believers so long as they continue at war.
39. The valley (or oasis) of Yathrib is sacred for the people of this document.
40. The 'protected neighbour' (of a believer) is (in respect of the right to protection) as the man himself, so long as he does no harm and does not act treacherously.
41. No woman is given 'neighbourly protection' without the consent of her people.
42. Whenever among the people of this document there occurs any 'disturbance' or quarrel from which disaster for (the people) is to be feared, it is to be referred to God and to Muḥammad, the Messenger of God. God is the most scrupulous and truest (fulfiller) of what is in this document.
43. No 'neighbourly protection' is given to Quraysh and those who help them.
44. Between (the people of this document?) is (mutual) 'help' against whoever attacks Yathrib suddenly (without provocation?).
45. Whenever (the believers) are summoned to conclude and accept (or live under) a treaty, they conclude and accept it; when in turn they summon (unbelievers) to a similar (treaty), they are bound (to observe it) towards (the unbelievers) except in the case of those who fight about religion. (Incumbent) on every man is their share from their side which is towards them.
46. The Jews of al-Aws, both their clients and themselves, are in the same position as belongs to the people of this document while they are thoroughly honourable in their dealings with the people of this document. Honourable dealing (comes) before treachery.
47. A person acquiring (? guilt) acquires it only against himself. God is the most upright and truest (fulfiller) of what is in this document. This writing does not intervene to protect a wrong-doer or traitor. He who goes out is safe, and he who sits still is safe in Medina, except who-

ever does wrong and acts treacherously. God is 'protecting neighbour' of him who acts honourably and fears God, and Muḥammad is the Messenger of God.

Note. This document is difficult to interpret in parts owing to the terseness of the language, and the use of pronouns where English requires nouns. Thus the last clause of §45 yields no reasonable meaning as it stands, and has not been satisfactorily explained. Interpretative additions have been indicated by parentheses. In some cases they are relatively certain; in others a slight doubt may remain.
The terms 'neighbourly protection', 'protected neighbour', 'client', etc., are used in accordance with the technical sense explained on p. 8. The word 'help' has been placed in inverted commas to indicate that it has the technical sense of warlike support in securing vengeance, etc.

NOTES

Abbreviations

EI[1], *EI*[2]: *Encyclopaedia of Islam*, first and second editions.
EI(S): *Shorter Encyclopaedia of Islam.*
GAL, *GALS*: see Chapter 9, note 11.
Islam and Integration: W. Montgomery Watt, *Islam and the Integration of Society*, London, 1961.
Mecca: W. Montgomery Watt, *Muhammad at Mecca*, Oxford, 1953.
Medina: W. Montgomery Watt, *Muhammad at Medina*, Oxford, 1956.
Prophet and Statesman: W. Montgomery Watt, *Muhammad Prophet and Statesman*, London, 1961.

In Qur'ānic references, where two verse numbers are given (separated by a stroke), the former is that of the Egyptian official edition and the latter the older European numbering. Where only one number is given, the two coincide.

Chapter One

1. A justification of these statements will be found in the author's *Muhammad Prophet and Statesman*, and also, more fully, in *Muhammad at Mecca.*
2. This position is argued for in *Muhammad at Medina*, 225-8. For the complete text see Appendix, pp. 130-4 above. Cf. also R. B. Serjeant, 'The "Constitution of Medina" ', *Islamic Quarterly*, viii (1964), 3-16.
3. Cf. *Exodus*, 21.23 f., etc., which are referred to in *Matthew*, 5.38.
4. Cf. Austin Kennett, *Bedouin Justice*, Cambridge, 1925, dealing with British administration in Sinai.
5. Alois Musil, *The Manners and Customs of the Rwala Bedouins*, New York, 1928, 493, etc.
6. Cf. Ignaz Goldziher, *Muhammedanische Studien*, Halle, 1888, i. 104-7; translated by S. H. Stern as *Muslim Studies*, i, London, 1968.

7. *Rwala Bedouins*, 451; the concept of protection is dealt with in pp. 438-54 and of vengeance in pp. 489-503.
8. Arthur Jeffery, *The Foreign Vocabulary of the Qur'ān*, Baroda, 1938, s.v.; Josef Horovitz, *Koranische Untersuchungen*, Berlin, 1926, 52.
9. Rudi Paret, art. 'Umma' in *EI(S)*.
10. Ibn-Saʿd, *Ṭabaqāt*, i/2.16 (§2); aṭ-Ṭabarī, *Annales*, i. 1561-8, from Ibn-Is'ḥāq, translated by Alfred Guillaume in *The Life of Muhammad*, London, 1955, 654-7.
11. Cf. Watt, *Medina*, 247, 360; the phrase 'party of God' (*ḥizb Allāh*), which is also found, is perhaps non-technical.
12. Cf. Watt, *Medina*, 141 f.
13. *The Arabs*, London, 1937, 125.
14. E.g. Musil, *Rwala Bedouins*, 504-661, esp. 506-40.
15. Cf. Watt, *Islam and Integration*, 65-7.
16. Cf. Watt, *Medina*, 105-17.

Chapter Two

1. 42.10/8; 4.59/62; 24.47/6-52/1.
2. 8.41/2; cf. *Medina*, 232, 255.
3. For the Pledge of Good Pleasure (*bayʿat ar-riḍwān*) cf. Watt, *Medina*, 50 f., 234.
4. Cf. *Medina*, 233.
5. Cf. *Medina*, 242, 356 f.
6. Cf. *Medina*, 357, no. 10.
7. Cf. *Medina*, 355 ff., nos. 4, 12, 15.
8. There is a list of nearly forty men in *Medina*, 366-8; cf. ib. 235-8. Sura 4.59/62 enjoins obedience not only to Muḥammad, but also to those in authority among the Muslims.
9. Cf. *Medina*, 190, 235.
10. Cf. *Medina*, 190.
11. *Das Leben Muhammeds*, Leipzig, 1930, 154; 'Bei einer rein geistigen Bewegung . . .'.
12. Cf. Watt, *Islam and Integration*, 174-8.
13. Cf. Bruce M. Borthwick, 'The Islamic sermon as a channel of political communication', *Middle East Journal*, xxi (1967), 299-313.

Chapter Three

1. Cf. aṭ-Ṭabarī, *Tafsīr*, on 2.30/28 (= i. 153 of old edition).
2. The treatment of Khalīfa in this and the following paragraphs is based on my article 'God's Caliph', *Minorsky Memorial Volume*, Cambridge, forthcoming.
3. Cf. Th. Nöldeke, etc. *Geschichte des Qorans*, Hildesheim, 1961,

iii. 210, n. 6. In Turkish the word and its variants mean a subordinate official.

4. Glaser, no. 618; quoted from R. Blachère, *Le Coran*, Paris, 1949, p. 241 (note on 38.26/5).
5. For the use of this title cf. Goldziher, *Muhammedanische Studien*, ii. 61 f., also in *Revue de l'Histoire des Religions*, xxxv (1897), 335-8; T. W. Arnold, *The Caliphate*, Oxford, 1924, 44 f., 51 f.; Watt, 'God's caliph'; Emile Tyan, *Institutions du Droit Public Musulman*, i, 'Le Califat', Paris, 1954; Armand Abel, 'Le Khalife, présence sacrée', *Studia Islamica*, vii (1957), 29-45.
6. Goldziher, in *RHR*, xxxv (1897), 331-5.
7. Cf. art. 'Amīr al-Mu'minīn' by Sir Hamilton Gibb in *EI*².
8. The tangle is being unravelled by recent studies, especially some made at Naples; see art. "ʿAlī' in *EI*² by Laura Veccia Vaglieri. An important study of the tendencies of historians is *ʿAlī and Muʿāwiya in early Arabic tradition*, by Erling Ladewig Petersen, Copenhagen, 1964.
9. Cf. Goldziher, *Muhammedanische Studien*, ii. 31.
10. The best general account for the topics covered is Henri Lammens, *Le Berceau de l'Islam*: *l'Arabie occidentale à la veille de l'hégire*; i (all published), 'Le climat, les bédouins', Rome, 1914. Most of the second half deals with the position of the *sayyid*. For modern parallels cf. Musil, *Rwala Bedouins*, 50 f., etc. Other useful articles are: Carlo A. Nallino, 'Sulla costituzione delle tribu arabe prima dell' Islamismo', in *Raccolta di scritti*, Rome, 1941, iii. 64-86; E. Bräunlich, 'Beitrage zur Gesellschaftsordnung der arabischen Beduinenstämme', *Islamica*, vi (1933/34), 68-111, 182-229; Joseph Henninger, 'La société bédouine ancienne', in F. Gabrieli (ed.), *L'antica società beduina*, Rome, 1949, 69-93.
11. For the early history of judicial administration cf. N. J. Coulson, *A History of Islamic Law*, Edinburgh, 1964, 21-35; J. Schacht, *An Introduction to Islamic Law*, Oxford, 1964, 15-27; Emile Tyan, *Histoire de l'organisation judiciaire en pays d'Islam*, Paris, 1938, i. esp. 98-138.
12. This view is expounded at greater length and with references in 'Shīʿism under the Umayyads', *Journal of the Royal Asiatic Society*, 1960, 158-72.
13. Pp. 123-5.

Chapter Four

1. Ibn-al-Athīr, *Kāmil*, Cairo, 1348, ii. 350 f. (A.H. 15). Cf. also *EI*², arts. "Aṭā'' (Cl. Cahen), 'Dīwān' *ad init.* (A. A. Duri), 'Djaysh', i (Cl. Cahen); *Islam and Integration*, 96.

2. Cf. Rudolf Veselý, 'Die Anṣār im ersten Bürgerkriege (36-40d.H.)' *Archiv Orientální*, xxvi (1958), 36-58.
3. Cf. the theorist al-Māwardī, *Al-aḥkām as-sulṭāniyya*, 351, French tr. 439. In practice there were some minor exceptions.
4. In *Modernization of the Arab World*, ed. J.H. Thompson and R.D. Reischauer, Princeton, 1966, 60, from an article 'The Rôle of the Army in the Traditional Arab State' (pp. 52-60).
5. Cf. *Medina*, 358-60; A. S. Tritton, *The Caliphs and their Non-Moslem Subjects*, Oxford, 1930.
6. Cf. *EI*², art. 'Dhimma' by Cl. Cahen.
7. Cf. A.H. Hourani, *Minorities in the Arab World*, London, 1947.
8. Cf. *EI*², arts. ''Āmil' (A.A. Duri), 'Amīr' (Cl. Cahen).

Chapter Five

1. Cf. Watt, 'Khārijite thought in the Umayyad Period', *Der Islam*, xxxvi (1961), 215-31; *Islam and Integration*, 94-104.
2. Cf. *Qur'ān*, 6.57; 12.40, 67; etc.
3. Cf. *Mecca*, 137-40.
4. Cf. *EI*², art. 'Azāriḳa' (R. Rubinacci).
5. Cf. *EI(S)*, art. 'Ibāḍīya' (T. Lewicki).
6. Cf. references in ch. 3, n. 12, and ch. 5, n. 1.
7. Cf. *EI*², art. 'Ḥanīf' (Watt).
8. *La Passion d'al-Hallaj*, Paris, 1922, i. 182-9, with materials for the early history of this use of *zandaqa*.

Chapter Six

1. Cf. Hamilton A. R. Gibb, *Studies on the Civilization of Islam*, London, 1962, esp. p. 14.
2. For 'the ancient schools of law' cf. Schacht, *Introduction to Islamic Law* and Coulson, *History of Islamic Law*; for the 'pious opposition' cf. J. Wellhausen, *The Arab Kingdom, and its fall*, Calcutta, 1927; for 'the general religious movement' cf. Watt, *Islamic Philosophy and Theology*, 30.
3. Cf. Watt, 'The Early Development of the Muslim Attitude to the Bible', *Transactions of the Glasgow University Oriental Society*, xvi (1957), 50-62, esp. §1; also *Islam and Integration*, 259 f.; and *EI*¹, art. 'Taḥrīf' (F. Buhl).
4. Cf. J.A.C. Brown, *Techniques of Persuasion: from Propaganda to Brainwashing*, Harmondsworth, 1963, 25.
5. Cf. Cl. Cahen, in von Grunebaum (ed.), *Unity and Variety in Muslim Civilization*, p. 142; but contrast p. 152.

6. The name *mujtahid* is given to al-Isfarā'inī (d. 1027) and al-Māwardī (d. 1058); cf. Ibn-Khallikān (tr. De Slane), i. 8, and Yāqūt, *Mu'jam*, v. 409. Al-Juwaynī (d. 1085) spoke as if a group of *ahl al-ijtihād* still existed (*Irshād*, ed. Cairo, 426).
7. Cf. Schacht, *Introduction to Islamic Law*, index, for the various points mentioned.
8. Cf. (a) *The Book of Knowledge*, tr. by Nabih Amin Faris, Lahore, 1962, especially section 4; (b) *The Faith and Practice of al-Ghazālī*, tr. W.M. Watt, London, 1953, esp. 55-8. For the following references to al-Ghazālī's career, cf. Watt, *Muslim Intellectual*, Edinburgh, 1963.
9. A general account is given in *EI*(*S*), art. 'Ṭarīḳa' (Louis Massignon); cf. also A. J. Arberry, *Sufism*, London, 1950, 84-92.
10. Cf. Henri Laoust, *Essai sur les doctrines sociales et politiques de Ibn Taimīya*, Cairo, 1939, 31.
11. Cf. Gibb, *Studies on the Civilization of Islam*, 28-32, esp. 31; also relationships between the religious institutions and the orders in the Ottoman empire, cf. H.A.R. Gibb and Harold Bowen, *Islamic Society and the West*, London, 1950, 1957, i/2, 179-206.

Chapter Seven

1. *EI*², art. ''Abd al-Ḥamīd b. Yaḥyā . . .' (H.A.R. Gibb); also Gibb, *Studies*, 63; cf. al-Mas'ūdī, *Murūj adh-Dhahab*, vi. 64, where Marwān II reads about the Persian kings.
2. There is now a full and authoritative study by Dominique Sourdel, *Le Vizirat 'Abbāside de 749 à 936*, Damascus, 1959-60. Cf. also S.D. Goitein, 'The Origin of the Vizierate and its True Character', reprinted from *Islamic Culture*, xvi (1942) in *Studies in Islamic History and Institutions*, Leiden, 1966, 168-96.
3. Cf. *EI*², art. 'Barāmika', chiefly by D. Sourdel.
4. Cf. F. Gabrieli, 'L'opera di Ibn al-Muqaffa'', *Rivista degli studi orientali*, xiii (1931-2), 197-247; Gerard Lecomte, *Ibn Qutayba*, Damascus, 1965, 184-9; F.R.C. Bagley, *Ghazālī's Book of Counsel for Kings*, London, 1964, lix-lxiv.
5. General accounts of the 'Mirrors'; Gustav Richter, *Studien zur Geschichte der älteren arabischen Fürstenspiegel*, Leipzig, 1932; Erwin I.J. Rosenthal, *Political Thought in Medieval Islam: an Introductory Outline*, Cambridge, 1958, 67-83; Bagley, *op. cit.*, esp. ix-xvi, lvi-lxxiv.
6. London, 1951.
7. London, 1960.

8. Translated by F. R. C. Bagley, as mentioned in a previous note; (Arabic title *Naṣīḥat al-Mulūk*); a rival *Sirāj-al-Mulūk* by aṭ-Ṭurṭūshī (d. 1126) is translated into Spanish.
9. Paris, 1954; 'Le livre de la couronne . . .'
10. Cf. H. A. R. Gibb, 'The Social Significance of the Shuubiya', reprinted in *Studies on the Civilization of Islam*, 62-73.
11. The contrast of the two blocs is worked out more fully in 'The Political Attitudes of the Muʿtazilah', *Journal of the Royal Asiatic Society*, 1963, 38-57, esp. 43-6. A similar distinction, though referring to a slightly later period, is made by Louis Massignon, *Passion d'al-Hallāj*, i. 204.
12. Cf. Watt, 'The Rāfiḍites', *Oriens*, xvi (1963), 110-21.
13. Petersen, *ʿAlī and Muʿāwiya in Early Arabic Tradition.*
14. Cf. Ch. Pellat, *Le Milieu Baṣrien et la Formation de Ǧāḥiẓ*, Paris, 1953, 188-94.
15. Cf. W. M. Patton, *Aḥmed b. Ḥanbal and the Miḥna*, Leiden, 1897.
16. Cf. Watt, 'Political Attitudes' (see note 11 above).

Chapter Eight

1. Reynold A. Nicholson, *A Literary History of the Arabs*, London, 1907, etc., 79.
2. Cf. EI^2, arts. '*dār al-ʿahd*' (H. Inalcik), '*dār al-ḥarb*' (A. Abel), '*dār al-islam*' (A. Abel), '*dār al-ṣulḥ*' (D. B. Macdonald, A. Abel); also M. Khadduri, *War and Peace in the Law of Islam*, Baltimore, 1955; id., *The Islamic Law of Nations, Shaybānī's Siyar*, Baltimore, 1966; M. Hamidullah, *Muslim Conduct of State*, Hyderabad, 1941/2.
3. Cf. Gardet, *Cité musulmane*, esp. 97 and index s.v. *āmān*; also Khadduri, *War and Peace*, 220 f.
4. See especially Wilfrid Cantwell Smith, *Islam and Modern History*, Princeton, 1957, 206-55.
5. Cf. EI^2, art. 'Hadīth' (J. Robson); H. A. R. Gibb, *Mohammedanism*, London, 1949, ch. 5, pp. 72-87.
6. Cf. Coulson, *History of Islamic Law*, 174-6.
7. Cf. Schacht, *Islamic Law*, 50-2; Coulson, *Islamic Law*, 128-32, etc.
8. Cf. Gibb and Bowen, *Islamic Society and the West*, i/1. 23 f.; Schacht, *Islamic Law*, 91 f.; Levy, *Social Structure of Islam*, 266-9.
9. Cf. Gardet, *Cité musulmane*, 185-7.
10. The brevity of the mention of rights in Gardet, *Cité musulmane*, 200, shows the minimal importance of this concept in Islam; cf. *ibid.*, 38, 93, 118.

11. Franz Rosenthal, *The Muslim Concept of Freedom*, Leiden, 1960, 122. Cf. Gardet, *Cité musulmane*, 69-72.
12. Louis Massignon's *Passion d'al-Hallāj*, Paris, 1922, is one of the most important works by an occidental Islamist in the present century. The first volume traces his career in its historical context and has useful political insights. The second volume, dealing with theology, is difficult to read, but is an invaluable store of references and suggestions. Part of chapter 12 (pp. 719-71) deals with politics.
13. Cf. pp. 55-9.
14. Cf. p. 128 below, and *Islam and Integration*, pp. 203-4.
15. Cahen in von Grunebaum (ed.), *Unity and Variety in Muslim Civilization*, p. 144.

Chapter Nine

1. Cf. *EI*², arts. ''Abbāsids' (B. Lewis, p. 18a), 'Aghlabids' (iii, ad. init.).
2. For the dynasties cf. C.E. Bosworth, *The Islamic Dynasties*, Edinburgh, 1967, pp. 99-106; or general histories of the Islamic world.
3. Cf. *EI*², art. 'Buwayhids' (C.C. Davies), also ''Abbāsids'.
4. Cf. *EI*², art. 'Atabak' (Cl. Cahen); A.H. Lybyer, *The Government of the Ottoman Empire in the time of Suleiman the Magnificent*, Cambridge, 1913, etc.
5. 'Al-Māwardī's Theory of the Khilāfah', *Islamic Culture* (Hyderabad), xi (1937), 291-302; reprinted in *Studies*, 151-65; see esp. p. 152 f.
6. *Studies*, 162.
7. *Archives d'histoire du droit oriental* (Paris), iii (1939), 401-10; reprinted in *Studies*, 141-50.
8. *Studies*, 148.
9. E. I. J. Rosenthal, *Political Thought in Medieval Islam*. A work in English dealing with selected writers is *Studies in Muslim Political Thought and Administration* by H.K. Sherwani, Lahore, 1942, etc.
10. Rosenthal, *Political Thought*, p. 114.
11. *GAL*, i. 177; *GALS*, i. 288. (These are abbreviations for the fundamental work of Arabic bibliography: Carl Brockelmann, *Geschichte der arabischen literatur*, second edition, Leiden, 1943, 1949, with three Supplementbänder, Leiden, 1937-42).
12. *GAL*, i. 207 f.: *GALS*, i. 345 f.
13. Cf. *Studies*, 144.
14. Cambridge, 1932; see esp. 192, art. 10.

15. A translation will be found in *A Commentary on the Creed of Islam* translated by E.E.Elder, New York, 1950, 141; the commentary on this article (pp. 141-51) by at-Taftazānī (d. 1389) is from an Ashʿarite standpoint. There is another translation in D.B.Macdonald, *Development, etc.*, 313 f. Cf. *GAL*, i. 548-50; *GALS*, i. 758-61.
16. Cf. *GAL*, i. 233 (section B); *GALS*, i. 376.
17. Cambridge, 1961, with an Introduction.
18. Cf. F.M.Najjar, 'Fārābī's Political Philosophy and Shīʿism', *Studia Islamica*, xiv. 57-72; also Watt, *Muslim Intellectual*, Edinburgh, 1963, 38-43.
19. Cf. *GAL*, i. 201; *GALS*, i. 324 f. A later creed is that translated by W.Ivanow as *A Creed of the Fatimids*, Bombay, 1936, esp. arts. 30-43.
20. *A Shiʿite Creed* (Islamic Research Association Series, No. 9), London, 1942, 89-100. Cf. *GAL*, i. 200 f.; *GALS*, i. 321 f.
21. Edition of Cairo, 1947, pp. 178-239; cf. *GAL*, i. 211; *GALS*, i. 349.
22. Cf. *GAL*, i. 589-99; *GALS*, i. 812-28; also Watt, *Muslim Intellectual*, 44 f.
23. Ed. Istanbul, 1928, pp. 270-94 (ch. 13); a brief statement may be found in his book on sects, *Al-farq bayn al-firaq*, translated by A.S.Halkin as *Moslem Schisms and Sects*, Tel-Aviv, 1935, 210-16. Cf. *GAL*, i. 482; *GALS*, i. 666 f.
24. Cf. *GAL*, i. 483; *GALS*, i. 668.
25. Cf. *GAL*, i. 502; *GALS*, i. 686.
26. Cf. *GAL*, i. 486-8; *GALS*, i. 671-3.
27. Cf. *GAL*, i. 535-46; *GALS*, i. 744-56. Watt, *Muslim Intellectual*, 74-86, etc. Of articles about al-Ghazālī there may be mentioned Leonard Binder, 'Al-Ghazālī and Islamic Government', *Muslim World*, xlv (1955), 229-41; Ann K.S.Lambton, 'The Theory of Kingship in the *Naṣīḥat al-Mulūk* of Ghazālī', *Islamic Quarterly*, i (1954), 47-55.
28. *The Nasirean Ethics*, translated from the Persian by G. M. Wickens, London, 1964.
29. *Al-Bābu'l-Ḥādī ʿAshar*, translated by W.McE.Miller, London, 1928, esp. pp. 61-81; this includes a commentary by Miqdād-i-Fāḍil (d. 1423). Cf. *GAL*, ii. 211 f.; *GALS*, ii. 206-9.
30. Cairo, 1939, esp. pp. 278-317.
31. *Le traité de droit public d'Ibn Taimīya*, translated by Henri Laoust, (vol. i), Beirut, 1948. Cf. *GAL*, ii. 125-7; *GALS*, ii. 119-26.
32. *Taḥrīr al-aḥkām fī tadbīr millat al-islām*; for details see *GAL*, 89; *GALS*, ii. 80 f.

33. *Ibn Khaldūn: The Muqaddimah*, translated by Franz Rosenthal, 3 vols., London, 1958, esp. ch. 3 (i. 311 to ii. 232).
34. London, 1839; cf. *EI*², art. '(al-) Dawānī' (A.K.S. Lambton) also *GAL*, ii. 281-4; *GALS*, ii. 306-9.
35. For the details, cf. Arnold, *Caliphate*, ch. 12.

Chapter Ten

1. Cf. Watt, 'Rāfiḍites'; also 'The Reappraisal of Abbasid Shi'ism' in *Arabic and Islamic Studies in Honor of Hamilton A.R. Gibb*, ed. G. Makdisi, Leiden, 1965, 638-54.
2. Abū-Ja'far al-Qummī (d. 903 – but perhaps confused with another Abū-Ja'far al-Qummī (d. 991) commonly known as ash-Shaykh aṣ-Ṣādūq); two men called an-Nawbakhtī (d. 923, 912); Sa'd ibn-'Abd-Allāh al-Ash'arī (d. c. 911); al-Kulīnī (d. 939), an important jurist. Cf. *GAL*, i. 199; *GALS*, i. 318-20; the earlier persons mentioned here doubtless discussed legal questions from a Rāfiḍite angle. General works are: R. Strothmann, *Die Zwölfer-Schī'a*, Leipzig, 1926; Dwight M. Donaldson, *The Shi'ite Religion*, London, 1933; also Strothman, art. 'Shī'a', in *EI(S)*. Cf. also above p. 106, no. 6 and p. 107, no. 15.
3. Cf. Edward G. Browne, *A Literary History of Persia*, Cambridge, 1953, etc. iv. 49-83, etc.
4. Cf. Leonard Binder, *The Ideological Revolution in the Middle East*, New York, 1964, 18, 135, 139.
5. Cf. Bernard Lewis, *The Origins of Ismā'īlism*, Cambridge, 1940; W. Madelung, 'Das Imamat in der frühen ismailitischen Lehre', *Der Islam*, xxxvii (1961), 43-135; M. Canard, art. 'Fāṭimids' in *EI*², with extensive bibliography. Cf. also P.J. Vatikiotis, *The Fatimid Theory of State*, Lahore, 1957; also p. 105, no. 5.
6. Cf. B. Lewis, *op. cit.*, 49-54.
7. Cf. Watt, *Islam and Integration*, 67-73; M.G.S. Hodgson, *The Order of Assassins*, 's-Gravenhage, 1955.
8. Cf. W. Ivanow, art. 'Ismā'īlīya' in *EI(S)*; A.A.A. Fyzee, art. 'Bohorās' in *EI*²; also forthcoming articles in *EI*².
9. Cf. R. Strothmann, *Das Staatsrecht der Zaiditen*, Strassburg, 1912; also art. 'Zaidīya' in *EI*¹ and *EI(S)*; Bosworth, *The Islamic Dynasties*, 71-73; W.M. Watt, in *The Saviour God*, ed. by S.G.F. Brandon, Manchester, 1963, 200-03.

Chapter Eleven

1. Cf. Albert Hourani, *Arabic Thought in the Liberal Age, 1798-1939*, London, 1962; Sylvia G. Haim (ed.), *Arab Nationalism*,

an Anthology, Berkeley, 1962; Wilfred Cantwell Smith, *Islam in Modern History*, Princeton, 1957; Jacques Berque, *The Arabs, their history and future*, London, 1964, esp. chapters 7 and 12, 'A contemporary imamate', 'Political values'.

2. In Haim, p. 100.
3. Cf. Sylvia Haim's 'Introduction' in *Arab Nationalism*, 58-64.
4. *Modern Trends in Islam*, Chicago, 1947, 115-17, etc.
5. What is here called 'solidarity' might be called by some 'a feeling of belonging together'. Cf. Cahen in *Unity and Variety* ed. von Grunebaum, 144, 'The sense of Muslim solidarity was a reality independent of the unity or disunity in the political system.'
6. Cf. Gardet, *Cité musulmane*, 331-43, 'La notion actuelle de démocratie et ses composantes'.
7. *Modern Egypt*, London, 1908, ii. 229.
8. *Jeremiah*, 6.16.
9. Cf. D.B.Macdonald, art. 'Mahdī' in EI^1; C. Snouck Hurgronje, 'Der Mahdi', *Verspreide Geschriften*, Bonn, 1923, i. 145-82.
10. Cf. *Islam in Tropical Africa*, ed. I.M.Lewis, London, 1966, p. 427 f.
11. See esp. P.M.Holt, *The Mahdist State in the Sudan*, Oxford, 1958.
12. View referred to in Gibb, *Modern Trends*, 117 f.
13. Esp. ch. 8, section 2, pp. 93-6.
14. The basic work is *Die arabischen Übersetzungen aus dem Griechischen*, by Moritz Steinschneider, Graz, 1960; reprinted from various periodicals, 1889-96.
15. Cf. EI^1, art. 'Ḳahwa' (C. van Arendonk).
16. London, 1934; based on earlier lectures in Madras and Oxford.

INDEX

The Arabic article al-, *with its variants such as* an-, ash-, *etc., is neglected in the alphabetical arrangement, except in the word Allāh. An asterisk indicates bibliographical data.*

al-ʿAbbās, 45
ʿAbbāsid(s) (dynasty)
army: decline of military power, 100; use of Turkish mercenaries, 19, 48, 100
autocratic methods, 39
caliphate: accession to, 45; decline of political power, 100; dissolution of, 34, 99, 100, 108; independent dynasties under, 99; suggestion of divine appointment, 34; titles under, 34
clients: pledged to remove grievances of, 90-1; support of regime, 78
descendants of, living in Cairo, 34
Islam, outward recognition of, 39
law under: desire for uniformity, 65-6, 126; recognition of 'ancient schools', 65
power struggle: decision to rely on constitutionalist bloc, 67, 110, 111; under first, 66-7, 82-5
religious institution: attitude to, 75; compromise with ulema, 75, 102; early recognition of, 39; retention of certain powers, 75, 102
Shīʿite support for, 45, 78, 110
Sunnism, commitment to, 111
Umayyads and: criticism of, 34; ousting of, 45
ʿAbd-Allāh ibn-az-Zubayr, 37, 55-6
Abd-an-Nasser, Gamal, 118
ʿAbd-Manāf, clan of, 38
Abel, A., 137*, 140*
Abraham, 89
abrogation, doctrine of, 94
Abū-Bakr (first caliph)
announcement on death of Muḥammad, 31
command of Syrian expedition, 18-19
designation of ʿUmar I as successor, 35, 36
relationship to Muḥammad 21, 32
succession question: chosen as caliph, 32; part in, 31; Shīʿite view of, 43, 86;

Abū-Bakr – *contd.*
superiority of, 87; wisdom of choice, 32
title of: *khalīfat rasūl Allāh*, 32, 34; reputed rejection of 'caliph of God', 33-4; vagueness of, 33
Abū-Ḥanīfa, 105
see also Ḥanafite school
Abū-Ja'far al-Qummī, 143
Abū-Lahab, 98
Abū-Ya'lā ibn-al-Farrā, 106*
Abū-Yūsuf, 105*
Achaemenian empire, 80
adab (belles-lettres), 70, 81
Adam, 33
adaptation
actualizing possibilities of, 123-9
creation of Sharī'a as, 125
effected by Muḥammad, 123-124
future, through intellectuals, 128-9
need for, 123
9th c. Sunnism as, 125
resistance to, 123
through appearance of charismatic leader, 123-5, 128, 129
through *ijmā'*, 127-8
through ulema and intellectuals, 125-7
through Mahdism, 124-5
Aden, 119
administration
administrative decisions: disinterestedness of ulema in, 96; effect of, 94-5; imperial decrees formulated from, 96; rise of practice, 41-2
adoption of Persian methods of, 29, 71
colleges for training in, 74-5
literature on art of, 81-2
Muḥammad's handling of details of, 25
provincial, 12, 41, 52, 53
Umayyad, based on pre-Islamic ideas, 39-40
see also secretaries
Afghanistan, 99
Affair of the Lie, 21-2
Africa(n)
East, 114
North: disappearance of Christianity from, 52; Muslim expansion through, 18
North-West, Almohad and Almoravid rule in, 124-5
socialism, 122
tropical, spread of Islam in, 25, 29, 59
West, Mahdist movement in, 124
Aga Khan, 114
Aghlabid dynasty, 99
agoranomos, 76, 95
agreements
Muḥammad's, with clans of Medina, 4
see also alliances
ahl adh-dhimma, *see* 'protected minorities'
ahl al-kitāb (people of the Book), 51
Ahl as-Sunna, 84
see also Sunnism
Aḥmad ibn-Ḥanbal, 72, 87
see also Ḥanbalite
Ahmadiyya (sect), 35
'Ā'isha
Affair of the Lie, 21-2
relationship to Abū-Bakr, 21, 32
Akaba, 49

Akkad, 80
Alamut, capture of, 114; also 107
Aleppo, 105
Algeria
  Ibāḍites in, 56
  independent dynasty in, 99
  membership of Arab League, 119
ʿAlī (ʿAlī ibn-Abī-Ṭālib)
  as caliph: Abū-Bakr's superiority to, 87; acclamation of, 36; Arbitration over, 37, 54; Muʿāwiya I's refusal to recognize, 37
  assassination of, 37, 38
  as the rightful imam, 111
  charisma of descendants of Fāṭima and, 110
  civil war between Muʿāwiya I and, 37, 43
  followers of, representing new nobility, 47
  imams: Alid, 86-7, 110-12; restricted to descendants of Fāṭima and, 45
  Khārijite revolts against, 54
  relationship to Muḥammad, 31, 36
  revolts of followers, 43
  Shīʾite: claims for, 31, 83, 86; Shīʿat ʿAlī, 43; view that Muḥammad designated as successor, 42-3
ʿAlī Zayn-al-ʿĀbidīn, 114
ʿAllāma-i-Ḥillī, 107*
alliance(s) (*ḥilf*, *taḥāluf*)
  administrative and financial aspects of, 25
  as non-aggression pacts, 13
  deputations requesting, 4, 13
  growth of system, 24-5
  limiting scope of razzias, 15, 16
  Muḥammad's: political effects of, 25, 26; with Iraqi tribes, 13-14; with Medinan clans, 4, 13; with nomadic tribes, 13, 24; with non-Muslims, 11; with polytheists, 11
  strengthening the group, 8, 13
  types of, 8, 13-14
  with Muḥammad as an individual, 24
Almohads, 124
Almoravids, 124-5
alms, legal, (*zakāt*) *see* tithe
American concept of religion, ix
ʿāmil (agent), 52
amīr (commander), 52
amīr al-muʾminīn (commander of the faithful), 34
amīr al-umarāʾ, 100
amr (command), 34
al-amr bi-l-maʿrūf . . ., 96
Anṣār (Muslims of Medina)
  benefit from principle of 'priority of Islam', 47
  consultation on succession to Muḥammad, 31
  consultation on succession to Muʿāwiya II, 39
    see also Medina
Antonius, George, 117*
Anūshirvān, 81
ʿanwatan, 50
apostasy (*ridda*)
  leading to expulsion, 63
  punishable by death, 62
  Wars of the, 64
Arab(s)
  arrogance, resentment at, 78, 83
  Christian, 119
  definition by descent, 117, 118

Arab(s) – *contd.*
implication that Egyptians are not, 117-18
Ishmael as ancestor of, 89
League: concept of, 118-19; total population of, 119
nationalism, 117, 119-20
what is an, 117-18
see also nomadic tribes, pre-Islamic Arabia
Arabic humanities, 69-70
Arabic language, 9-11, 27, 29, 33, 39, 54, 60, 69, 81, 88, 100, 117
Arabism
deficient in political conceptions, 79
pan-, potentialities of, 118-19
Aramaeans, 78, 83
Arberry, A. J., 139*
arbiter(s) (*ḥakam*)
confined to civil and secular matters, 26
demise of office, 41
denunciation of those rejecting decisions of, 24
disputes referred to, 40-1
Muhammad as, 21, 26
role of, in pre-Islamic Arabia, 20, 40-1
Arbitration
ʿAlī's association with, 37, 54
Khārijite view of, 54
on the succession question, 37-8
Aristotle, 104
army
administration through, 52
admission of non-Arabs, 47-8
as guardians of the nation's morals, 49
composition of, 47-8
inducc ɛnts to recruit, 48
in Tabūk expedition, 25
methods of retaining fighting strength, 18
professional, 48, 100
register of those serving, 46-7
service confined to Muslims, 19, 48-9
use of Turkish mercenaries, 19, 48, 100
Arnold, T. W., 137*
asceticism, Persian, 83
al-Ashʿarī
defence of Sunnism, 127
political writings of, 105*
Ashʿarite
political theory: collapse of, 102; development of views, 106
theology: contrast with Māturīdite school, 105; school of, 85; Seljūq's use of, 101
Asia, spread of Islam in South-East, 59
see also Central Asia
Assassins, 114
astrology, 71, 126
astronomy, 126
atābeg (tutor-guardian), 101
autocratic
bloc: belief in charismatic leader, 88; composition of, 82-4; Hārūn ar-Rashīd's reliance on, 85; historical arguments, 86; Persian element in, 83; Rāfiḍites' support of, 110; secretaries' support of, 67, 82; Shīʿite element in, 83-4, 110
form of vizierate, 80
methods of ʿAbbāsids, 39
Averroes (Ibn-Rushd), 104

Avicenna (Ibn-Sīnā)
  Neoplatonism of, 71, 106, 127
  political thought, 104, 106*
Aws (tribe), 21
Ayla, 49
Azāriqa, 55-6
Az'har, 129
Azraqites (Azāriqa), 55-6

Badr, battle of
  enhancing Muḥammad's prestige, 22
  prestige of men of, 22
  stipends paid to those who fought at, 47
  victory against Meccans, 15
Badr-ad-Dīn ibn-Jamāʿa, 107*
Baghdad
  Buwayhid capture of 74, 100
  college in, 74
  effect of removal of capital to, 79, 82
  Fāṭimid rule in, 113
  Mongol sack of in 1258, 100, 107
  Seljūq capture of, 74, 100
al-Baghdādī, 106*
Bagley, F. R. C., 139*
Bahrein, Carmathian state of, 112-13; also 119
al-Bāqillānī, 106*
baraka, 39
Barmakids
  training of secretaries, 80
  under Hārūn ar-Rashīd, 85
Basra, Azraqite activities in, 55, 56
bayʿa (acclamation), 35, 86, 136
Baybars, 108
Bedouin, 8
Beirut, 117
believers, see *mu'minūn*
belles-lettres
  Persian themes in, 81
  rise of, 70
Berbers, 47-8, 119
Bergson, 129
Berque, J., 144*
Bible, 70, 72, 89
  see also New Testament, Old Testament
Bidpai, 81
Binder, L., 142*, 143*
Blachère, R., 137*
blackening of the face, 8
blood-wit
  agreement about amount of, 9
  among Rwala tribe, 7
  as alternative to *lex talionis*, 7, 9
  calculation of, 7
  failure to agree on, 21
  in case of allied polytheists, 11-12
  introduction into Arabia, 7
  recommendations to induce acceptance of, 9
  responsibility of kinship group for, 5, 8-9
body politic
  as federation of tribes, 14
  as 'super-tribe', 14
  creation of Islamic, 4
  establishment of new, from Medinan alliances, 4
  Muḥammad's message addressed to, 27
  political potentialities of Qur'ānic ideas realized in, 4
  relevance of pre-Islamic ideas to, 12-13
  tribe as, 12, 14
  type of alliance making tribes part of, 13
  see also state
Bohorās, 114

Book, People of, 11
booty
  as the primary aim of *jihād*, 17, 18
  conception of *jihād* modifying, 17-18
  division of, in larger expeditions, 46
  dīwān system, 46-7
  fifth part paid to treasury, 42, 46
  portion allotted in Islamic times, 22-3, 42
  portion allotted in pre-Islamic times, 22-3
  realization of conquests by Islamic state, 18
Borthwick, B., 136*
Bosworth, C. E., 141*
Bowen, H., 139*
Bräunlich, E., 137*
Britain, British, 19, 92, 124
Brockelmann, C., 141*
brotherhood
  continuing solidarity of tribe, 97
  reality of, of all Muslims, 120
  sense of, in Islam, 97
Brown, J. A. C., 138*
Browne, E. G., 143*
Buddhism, Buddhists
  as a political force of the future, ix
  as 'protected minorities', 51
Buhl, F., 26, 136*, 138*
al-Bukhārī, 93
Burjī Mamlūks, 101
Buwayhids (Būyids)
  appointment by caliph, 100
  capture of Baghdad, 74, 100
  defence of caliph against, 102
  difficulty of regarding them as guarantors of the Sharīʿa, 103
  recognition of Shīʿite legal rite, 111
  Shīʿite views of, 101, 103, 111
  succeeded by Seljūqs, 113
  support of Imamite jurists, 111
Byzantine, Byzantium
  account of emperor, 12
  agoranomos, 76, 95
  Meccan contacts with, 12
  suggested origin of 'protected minorities', 50
  tradition, Islamic disregard for, 81

Cahen, Cl., xi*, 137*, 138*, 141*
Cairo, 34, 102, 113
caliph(s)
  administrative powers of, 41-2, 75, 94-5
  advantage over *sayyid*, 41
  appointment of *ʿāmils*, 41, 52
  as head of the state, 42
  Cairene, 100
  difficulty of access to, 79
  divine appointment of, 33, 34
  financial powers of, 42
  judicial powers of, 41, 76
  lack of prophethood, 42
  leadership in war, 41
  religious duties of, 42
  subordination of war lords to, 100, 101, 102
  title of: 'caliph of God', 33-4; *khalīfat rasūl Allāh*, 33, 34; later uses of, 34-5, 108
Caliphate
  ʿAbbāsid: accession to, 45; dissolution of, 34, 99, 100, 108; independent dynasties under, 99
  after 1258, 107-9

Caliphate – *contd.*
as the symbol of the superiority of the Shariʿa, 102
Congress, 109
demise of, creating problems for the theorists, 108
nature of the, 40-2
Ottoman: abolition of, 35, 109; adoption of, 34-5, 108; Muslim recognition of, 108-9; resurrection of, 108
potential emotional appeal of new, 109
rāshidūn: as the golden age of the, 36; standard account of the accession of the, 35-6
study of the history of, 70
succession to, 35-40
the early, 31-45
Umayyad: form of succession practised by, 37-8; retention of, 39-40
Camel, battle of the, 38
camp cities
rise of, 48
settlement of civilians in, 52
Canard, M., 143*
Carmathians, 112, 113
Caspian Sea, 115
Catholic Christianity, mediaeval dominance of, 72-3
Central Asia, 52, 101, 117
Chad, 119
charisma (*baraka*)
see community, leadership
Chicago, 119
Chinese, 126
Christianity
as a future political force, ix
belief in the old paths, 123
contrast between 'church' and 'world' in, 29
conversion from, to Islam, 51, 70
conversion to, from Islam, 62-3
'corruption theory', 69, 70, 72
cultural contacts with Islam, 68
disappearance from North Africa and Central Asia, 52
extra ecclesia nulla salus, 59
historical traditions, Islamic disinterestedness in, 70-1, 72
intellectual superiority of Islam over, 71
mention of New Testament in Qur'ān, 49
Messianic idea, 44
Muslim contacts with, 69
place of Nicene creed in, 61
political involvement of, 26-7
question of acceptance of Muḥammad as Messenger of God, 49
replacement of Hellenistic systems, 68
toleration in, 51
under Ottoman empire, 52
working of Islamic religious institution and, 64
Christians
Arab, 119
'protected minorities': benefit of, 51; enhancement of self-esteem through, 18; option of joining, 16
referred to as community, 10
treaties with, 49
clans
formation of, on Islamic basis, 57

clans – *contd.*
  Medinan: alliances with nomads, 13; Muḥammad's alliances with, 4, 13
  Muḥammad as clan chief, 21
  responsibility for blood-wit, 5
  use of term, 11
clients (*mawālī*, sing. *mawlā*)
  ʿAbbāsids pledged to remove grievances of, 90-1
  arrogance of tribes towards, 78
  attachment to groups as, 7-8
  confederates and, 8
  non-Arabs becoming, on accepting Islam, 8, 61, 78
  resentment at status of, 78, 83
  support of ʿAbbāsids, 78
coffee drinking, 128
commander of the faithful, 34
commerce
  Meccan, 3
  prosperity leading to social malaise, 4
communal solidarity
  affecting spread of Islam, 29
  against crime, 5
  against unbelievers, 5, 9
  effect of, and Muḥammad's political power, 29
  hijra aiding realization of, 30
  ijmāʿ: as aspect of, 127-8; in external relations, 16 expressed in, 98
  Islam restoring, 28-9
  maintenance of, over centuries, 62-3
  protection under, 6, 9
  reality of, 28, 120, 123
  sense of: exerting pressure to conform, 98; fostering of, 30; independent of political systems, 98
  tension between individualism and, 97-8
community
  as a natural community, 62-3
  as bearer of values, 90-8
  Azraqite view of, 55-6
  charismatic: as the whole body of Muslims, 58-9; avoiding mistakes, 57; belief in, 98; Khārijite view of, 55, 56-7, 85; political aspect of, 59; Sharīʿa maintaining, 103; Sunnite belief in, 85; ulema's interest in maintaining, 102-3
  definition of: as believers, 12; decreasing need for specific name for, 12; in Constitution, 5, 9-10; in Qur'ān, 10
  devotion to, 59
  local, 14
  membership of: attainment of significance through, 57, 90; cessation of, 62; conditions of, 59-63; confession of faith as criterion of, 60, 61; consideration of, 54-63; defined in religious terms, 59-60; importance of, to Muslims, 55; involving element of intellectual belief, 56; religious significance of, 28; restricted to Arabs, 61; wider, of true believers, 57-9
  natural, *qawm* denoting nature of the, 9-14
  nature and purpose of, 90-2
  protection in, 55
  Sharīʿa conferring nobility on, 91

community – *contd.*
sin and exclusion from:
Khārijite views, 55, 56, 61; Murji'ite view, 58; practical effects of, 58-9; reluctance to expel from, 63
the individual and, 96-8
tribal concepts and, 12, 20
words and phrases denoting, 11, 12
zeal for, 59
see also umma
Companions (of Muḥammad), 43, 66
complaints, investigation of, 76, 95
confederation, 8
confession of faith
as criterion of believer, 60
attempts to make authoritative, 61-2
expressing acceptance of the values of Islam, 63
formula of, 60
history of, 60-1
conquest
dīwān making possible, 47
submission after fighting, 46, 50
voluntary submission, 46, 50
consensus, see *ijmāʿ*
Constantine, Donation of, 87
constitution, question of an Islamic, 121
constitutionalist bloc
ʿAbbāsid decision to rely on, 85, 110
Arab interest in, 84
belief in government in accordance with the Sharīʿa, 88
composition of, 84-5
rulers' realization of advantages of, 87
surrender to, 67, 88-9
ulema class interest in, 84
Constitution of Medina
amplified by the Qur'ān, 9
as a conflation of two documents, 4-5
as rooted in mentality and mores of pre-Islamic Arabs, 5-6, 10
character of, 5-6
compilation of, 5
concept of protection in, 8-9
date of, 5
essential points defining nature of state, 5
Muḥammad's position under, 20-3
references to Muḥammad in, 21
significance of, 4
text of, 130-4
use of *umma* in, 5, 9-10
consultation
defects of system, 79
in succession matters, 35, 37, 38, 39, 41
conversions
from Islam, 62-3
to Islam, 51, 70
Coulson, N. J., 137*
council of notables
defects of system for administration, 79
matters decided by tribal, 20, 40
courtier, rise of the, 79
createdness of the Qur'ān
declaration of belief in doctrine of, 73, 87
political relevance of doctrine, 88
creeds, 61-2
see also confession of faith

crime
avoidance of punishment of religious, 62
communal solidarity against, 5
kinship group's responsibility, 9
Murji'ite justification of punishment of, 58-9
police jurisdiction on, 76, 95
provisions of Constitution dealing with, 5
theologians' view of, 58-9
Cromer, Lord, 123, 144*
culture, Arabic, as a criterion of the Arab, 118
custom
Muḥammad following pre-Islamic, 66
Umayyads following pre-Islamic, 65

Damascus
as capital of the Umayyads, 37, 39, 41
repayment of tribute when protection ceased, 49-50
settlement of Muslims in, 52
dār al-ḥarb, 91
dār al-islām, 91
Darius, 80
Darke, H., 82*
dates as tribute, 46, 49
David, 33
Davies, C. C., 141*
Dawānī, 103, 107*
Daylam, Zaydite state in, 115
decision(s)
administrative: disinterestedness of ulema in, 96; effect of, 94-5; imperial decrees ormulated from, 96; rise practice of, 41-2
implementing Qur'ānic commands, 26
in tribal council, 40
judicial: basis of, under *qāḍī*, 42; denunciation of those rejecting, 24
legal: independent, 73; to be based on the Traditions, 66
Muḥammad's: acceptance of, 23, 26; implementing Qur'ānic prescriptions, 23-4; increasing use of, 26
'no decision but God's', 54
political, to be based on Qur'ān, 54
Qur'ānic sanction for, 23
declarations
increasing Muḥammad's power, 24-5
nature of, 24
of doctrine of createdness of the Qur'ān, 73, 87
decrees
practice of issuing legislative, 96
use of *qānūn*, 96
democracy
constitution in accordance with Sharī'a, 121
impersonality of modern, 120
personal element in Arab politics, 120-1
question of an Islamic constitution, 121
tribal, 120
Deputations, Year of, 13
deputations (*wufūd*)
consulted concerning succession to Mu'āwiya 11, 39
seeking alliance with Muḥammad, 13

dervish orders
  partial recognition of, 77
  rise of, 76
  Shah Ismāʿīl acknowledged head of, 112
designation (*naṣṣ*)
  imamate conferred by, 113
  in succession matters, 35, 37, 39, 86
deviants, pressure on, to conform, 121
dhikr, 77
dhimma (protection)
  defined, 49, 50
  see also 'protected minorities'
Dieterici, F., 105*
dīn (religion), 29
dīnī wa-dunyawī, 29
discussion
  expressed in religious terms, 64-5
  rise of, 64
  social and political relevance of, 65
dishonour, protection and, 8, 51
disputes
  referred to: arbiter, 20, 40-1; caliphs, 41; God and Muḥammad, 21, 22, 41; provincial governors, 41; *sayyid*, 40
Dīwān of ʿUmar
  breakdown of system, 48
  effect of, 47
  introduction of, 46
  list of stipends, 47
Donaldson, D. M., 143*
Donation of Constantine, 87
Dunlop, D. M., 105*
Duri, A. A., 137*, 138*

economic life of Mecca, 4
education
  Az'har university, 129
  content of, 67-8
  establishment of colleges, 74-5
  European pattern of Muslim, 117, 128-9
  jurisprudence as core of, 67
Egypt
  attempt to develop nationalism, 118
  dervish orders in, 77
  Fāṭimid rule in, 112-13
  Greek intellectual heritage of intellectuals of, 126
  implication that Egyptians are not Arabs, 117-18
  independence of, 118
  intellectual contacts through conquest, 68
  Islamic constitution of, 121
  membership of Arab League, 119
  Parliament, 116
Elath, 49
Elder, E. E., 142*
Emigrants from Mecca
  activities spoken of as *jihād*, 16
  as the most powerful clan in Medina, 24
  distinction between Medinan Muslims and, 15, 22, 130
  Muḥammad as military leader of, 22
  Muḥammad as *sayyid* of, 21
  occupation of, 15
  part in razzias, 15-16, 22
  those with status of emigrant added to, 24
emigrant status, 24
emir of emirs, 100
Empire, organization of, 46-53
Ethiopia, Meccan contacts with, 12

ethnic group
  concept of, in early Islam, 11
  umma as applied to, 10
European
  Christians under Ottomans, 52
  concept of religion as personal piety, ix
  contrast in political development, 64
  education, influence of, 117, 128-9
  élite, slowness to develop Arab consciousness, 118
  ideas, acceptance of, 116-17
  institutions, imitation of, 116
  scientific thought, assimilation of, 128-9
excommunication of hypocrites, 25
expansion
  as development of the razzia, 17, 18
  concept of protection leading to, 17
  early Islamic, 17
  methods by which achieved, 18
  Muḥammad's appreciation of centrality of need for, 18-19
  political concepts presupposing, 91-2
expeditions, *see* razzia
external affairs
  Muḥammad as autocrat in, 26
  responsibility of *sayyid* for tribal, 40

Fagnan, E., 105*
faith (*īmān*)
  kufr as opposite to, 62
  meaning of, in Islam, 60
Falāsifa, 127
families, family
  agents of hidden imams not members of, 45
  appointment of ʿAlīd imams, 110
  qualities of leadership inherent in certain, 35, 39, 44
  retention of caliphate in Umayyad, 39
  Shīʿite: belief in leadership inherent in, 110; view of inheritance of special powers, 44
  vague definition of in Umayyad period, 45
  Zaydite theory of claim from, 114
al-Fārābī
  Neoplatonism of, 71, 81
  political writings of, 104
  Shīʿite associations of, 105, 106
  superiority of argumentation, 127
  'The Virtuous City', 105*, 107
Faris, N. A., 139*
Fāṭima (daughter of Muhammad), 43, 45
Fāṭimids
  centralization of government, 113
  claim to be rightful imams, 102, 113
  concept of autocratic imam, 113
  form of Ismāʿīlite Shīʿism, 105-6, 112-13
  inability to support Ismāʿīlite movement, 113-14
  rule in: Baghdad, 113; Egypt, 102, 112-13

Fāṭimids – *contd.*
  state in Tunisia, 34, 112-13
  use of title of caliph, 34
federation
  as strengthening the group, 8
  confederate and client, 8
  Muḥammad's power as head of, 25
  of kinship groups, *umma* denoting, 11
  of tribes, body politic denoting, 14
  of tribes in alliance with Muḥammad, 13
  tribes consulted in caliphate succession, 39
  types of, 8
Fertile Crescent, 51
finance
  administration of in the provinces, 52
  'āmil as officer responsible for, 52
  caliph's powers, 42
  provincial governor's powers, 42, 52
  reform of the Dīwān, 46-7
  sources of, 42
Firdawsī, 83
firqa nājiya, 90
foreign policy
  jihād as unsatisfactory basis for, 19, 91, 92;
  'spheres' inapplicable to, 91
France, 17
freedom, concept of (*ḥurriyya*)
  absence from political thinking, 96
  combination of ideas performing function of, 97
  reasons for absence of, 96-7
Fulani empire, 124

Gabrieli, F., 137*, 139*
Gardet, L., xi*
Gaudefroy-Demombynes, M., xi*
geography, study of, 70
Germany, 121
al-Ghazālī
  Counsel for Kings, 82*
  defence of the caliphate, 106
  mastery of teaching of the Philosophers, 127
  on *takfīr*, 62
  rejection of Greek metaphysics, 127
  use of logical methods, 71, 127
  view of perversion of scholarship, 76
  writings of, 76, 106*
Gibb, Sir Hamilton, 102, 103-4, 105, 119, 137*, 138*, 139*, 140*, 144*
Glubb, Sir John Bagot, 49
Goitein, S. D., 139*
Goldziher, I., 135*, 137*
governor, provincial
  disputes referred to, 41
  duties of, 52-3
  financial powers of, 42
  selection of subordinates, 52
  titles applied to, 52
grammar, study of Arabic, 69
Greek
  culture: incorporation into Islamic world-view, 68, 71; refusal to acknowledge, 80-1
  metaphysics, rejection of, 127
  philosophy: acceptance of, 81; adaptation of, 126-7; translation of, 71; use of, 88
  thought, use of technical aspects of, 127

groups
attachment to as clients, 7-8
devices for increasing strength of, 7, 8
kinship, *see* kinship
Guillaume, A., 136*
guilt, solidarity of group in sharing, 7

ḥadīth, *see* Tradition
Haim, S., 143*
ḥakam, *see* arbiter
ḥalīf, *see* confederation
Halkin, A. S., 142*
al-Ḥallāj, 62, 98
ḥamāsa (fortitude), 90
Ḥamdānid (dynasty), 105
Hamidullah, M., 140*
Ḥanafite school of law, 66, 105
see also Abū-Ḥanīfa
Ḥanbalite school of law, 66
see also Aḥmad ibn-Ḥanbal
ḥanīf, 60
Ḥanīfite religion, Islam called, 60
Hārūn ar-Rashīd, 85
al-Ḥasan (son of ʿAlī)
as second imam, 111
attempt to gain caliphate, 43
al-Ḥasan ibn-aṣ-Ṣabbāḥ, 113-14
Hāshim, clan of
charisma of leadership in other branches of, 45
representing new nobility, 47
Shīʿite claim of special powers for, 43, 110
Hellenistic thought, 68; *see also* Greek
'help'
as sacred duty of the group, 6, 131, 132, 134
devices for extending circle of those obliged to, 7-8
in exacting revenge, 6-7
Jews and Muslims to render when necessary, 5
required for public security, 6
Henninger, J., 137*
heredity
Shīʿite view of transmission of special powers through, 44
Umayyad claim to leadership through, 38, 39
Hijra
aiding realization of communal solidarity, 30
Constitution dating from, 5
marking beginning of Muḥammad's political activity, 4
status of emigrant conferred on those who did not make, 24
use by Khārijites, 55
ḥilf, *see* alliance
Hinduism
as a political force in the future, ix
protected minorities from, 51
history
as still alive in Islam, ix
historical: ideas of the power struggle, 86-7; discussion arising from contemporary politics, 86
Imāmite rewriting of, 111
importance of, to Islam, ix
political ideas operative in, x
political theory expressed in form of, 36-7
pre-Islamic view of, 68
purpose in rewriting, 86
Shīʿite rewriting of, 43
study: of Arabia, 69; of the caliphate, 70
Hitler, 121

ḥizb Allāh (party of God), 136
Hodgson, M. G. S., 143*
Holt, P. M., 144*
holy war
  as a misleading description, 18
  see jihād
Horovitz, J., 136*
Hourani, A. H., 138*, 143*
al-Ḥudaybiya, treaty of, 23, 47
Hulagu, 107
humanism, ix
Ḥunayn (battle of)
  effect on Muḥammad's political power, 13
  significance of, 4
Hurgronje, C. Snouck, 144*
ḥurr, *see* freedom
al-Ḥusayn (son of ʿAlī)
  association with Zaydism, 114
  as third imam, 111
  attempt to gain caliphate, 43
hypocrites, excommunication of, 25

Ibāḍites (sect), 56
Ibn-al-Athīr, 70, 71, 137*
Ibn-Ḥanbal, *see* Aḥmad ibn-Ḥanbal
Ibn-Jamāʿa (Badr-ad-Dīn), 107*
Ibn-Khaldūn, 103, 107*
Ibn-al-Muqaffaʿ, 81, 82
Ibn-Rushd, *see* Averroes
Ibn-Saʿūd, 30
Ibn-Sīnā, *see* Avicenna
Ibn-Taymiyya, 107*
Ibn-Tūmart, 124
Ibn-az-Zubayr, *see* ʿAbd-Allāh ibn-az-Zubayr
ideals
  and laws, 92-6
  Traditions as expression of Islamic, 93
ideational
  aspect of the power struggle, 88-9
  system, *see* world-view
ideology, with functions of religion, ix
idolatry, 62, 63
ijmāʿ (consensus)
  adaptation through, 127-8
  as aspect of communal solidarity, 98, 127
  ratifying events, 102
  strength of, 128
ijtihād (independent judgement), 73, 94;
  see also mujtahid
ʿilm (knowledge), 41
imam(s), *imām*
  ʿAlid, recognized as heads of families, 110-11
  designation by predecessors, 86, 113
  hidden: agent for, 45, 111, 113; normal that imam be, 113; political implications of, 44-5; rendering regime *de facto* not *de iure*, 45; revival of idea, 111; Shīʿite conception of, 44; twelfth ʿAlid regarded as, 111; Zaydite rejection of doctrine of, 114-15
  Ismāʿīlite concept of, 113
  restricted to descendants of ʿAlī and Fāṭima, 45
  Shah of Persia regarded as reincarnation of, 112
  Shīʿite: list of twelve, 86-7; view of special powers of, 43-4
  trustee, 113
  Zaydite view of, 114-15

Imām al-Ḥaramayn, 106
imamate
  political writings on, 106-7
  sections on in treatises on theology, 105
Imāmism, *see* Imāmite party
Imāmite party (or sect)
  Buwayhid support for, 111
  known as the Twelvers or Ithnāʿashariyya, 111
  'moderate' Shīʿism and, 110-12
  official religion of Persia, 111-12, 117
  political doctrine of, 111
  rise of, 110-11
īmān, *see* faith
imperialism, concept of nationalism in struggle against, 117
Inalcik, H., 140*
independence
  of dynasties under caliphs, 99, 100
  part played by European-educated Muslims in, 117
  strengthening concept of Arab nationalism, 119
  through military force, 125
India
  Ismāʿīlites in, 114
  problem of Muslims in, 92
  refusal of Muslims to join Sultan's *jihād*, 19
individual(s)
  activities influenced by religion, 28
  community and, 96-8
  pressure to conform, 98
  religion and morality of, 28
  treatment of deviant, 97-8
inheritance, absence of law of primogeniture, 35, 101
Injīl (gospel), 49
  see also New Testament
injury, vengeance for, 9
Inquisition (Miḥna)
  Aḥmad ibn-Ḥanbal's refusal of, 87
  as conformity through force, 98
  effect on power struggle, 85, 87
  effect on ulema, 73, 74
  failure of, 85, 87, 88
inspector of the markets, 76, 95
intellectual(s)
  ʿAbbāsid recognition of religious, 39
  achievement in elaborating world-view, 69
  adaptation of Greek thought and science, 126-7
  adaptation through, 125-7
  future adaptation through, 77, 128-9
  ʿilm of, 41
  Islam replacing Christian intellectual systems, 68
  leaders emerging from discussion, 65
  outlook, creation of a homogeneous, 63
  role of ulema, 67
  stages in assimilation process, 127
  superiority of Islamic over Christian, 71
  systematizing Sharīʿa as effort of, 126
internal order, 19
investigation of complaints, 76, 95
Iqbal, Sir Mohammad, 129*, 144*
Iran, Iranian, 83, 117
  see also Persia

Iraq
attempt to develop local nationalism, 118
cultural heritage, 78
effect of shift of government to, 82
expansion into, through alliances, 17
Greek intellectual heritage of educated men of, 126
inhabitants becoming Muslims, 48
intellectual contacts through conquest of, 68
Meccan trade with, 3
membership of Arab league, 119
Muḥammad's alliances with tribes of, 13-14
Ireland, ix
Isaac, 89
Ishmael, 89
islām, meaning of, 60
Islam
ʿAbbāsids' recognition of, 39
absence of contrast between 'church' and 'world' in, 29
absence of political relevance of early, 3
acceptance of: as a political decision, 16-17; by seeking protection, 16; under alliance, 13
and occidental political ideas, 116-23
and the sword, 16
as a political force of the future, ix
called the Ḥanīfite religion, 60
development of Shīʿite, 110-15
hijra contributing to political unity of, 30
in contemporary politics, 116-29
'Islam reformed is no longer Islam', 123
Islamic socialism, 122
lack of success in political field, 29
less distinction between religious and secular in, 29
relevance to political and social organization, 28
Ismāʿīl, Shah of Persia, 111-12
Ismāʿīl, son of Jaʿfar aṣ-Ṣādiq, 112
Ismāʿīlite(s), Ismāʿīlīs
as revolutionary Shīʿism, 112-14
claim to rule over all Muslims, 113
concept of imam, 112, 113
Fāṭimid: followers of, 112-13; form of Shīʿism, 105-6
al-Ḥasan ibn-aṣ-Ṣabbāḥ as effective head of Eastern, 113-14
in India, 114
known as Seveners, 111, 112
movement in Syria and Persia, 113
seizure of power in Bahrein, 112-13
subsequent history of, 114
Ithnāʿashariyya, Ithnāʿasharites, *see* Imāmite party
Ivanow, W., 142*

Jaʿfar (brother of ʿAlī), 45
Jaʿfar aṣ-Ṣādiq, 110, 111, 112
Jaʿfarī legal rite, 111
jāhadū (strive, engage in *jihād*), 15, 16
al-Jāḥiẓ, 82, 87

Jalāl-ad-Dīn Dawānī (ad-Dawwānī), 103, 107*
jamā'a (community), 12, 84
jār, *see* 'neighbourly protection'
Jeffery, A., 136*
Jerusalem, 37, 38
Jesus, political aspects of teaching, 26-7
Jews
- Arabic-speaking, 118
- at Khaybar accepted in Pax Islamica, 49
- attitude to Muslim use of *umma*, 10
- conception of Messiah compared with Mahdism, 44, 124
- conversion of Muslims to Judaism as apostasy, 62
- enhancement of self-esteem through protection, 18
- Medinan: as a natural community, 11; attitude to Islam, 68; expulsion of clans, 5; groups remaining, 5; treaty with Muḥammad, 49
- Muslims' hostility to, 68-9
- of Maqnā, treaty with, 49
- option of becoming 'protected minority', 16
- punishment of clan of Qurayẓa, 22
- referred to as community, 10
- refusal to accept Muḥammad as Messenger of God, 49
- retention of own religion, 5
- survival of 'protected minorities', 52
- theory of corruption of Jewish scriptures, 69
- to render 'help' when necessary, 5
- Torah of, 49
- tribute paid by conquered, 46, 49
- Zionist, 118

Jihād, *jihād*
- absence of religious motive from, 17
- abuses of, 15, 19
- activities of Emigrants referred to as, 16
- and military service confined to Muslims, 48-9
- as a development of the razzia, 18
- as inner self-discipline, 19
- association with 'spheres', 91
- change in character of, 19
- conception of: influencing razzias, 17-18; introducing expanding sphere of protection, 17-18; modifying practice of hunting booty, 17
- concept of protection and extension of, 16-17
- direction of, leading to empire, 18-19
- 'holy war' as misleading description of, 18
- importance in Islamic expansion, 14
- in the way of God, 16
- later use of, 19
- Mahdist, 125
- meaning of, 16
- new theological views propounded to start, 19
- of 1914, 19
- period of importance of, 19
- proclaimed by Usuman, 124
- razzias and, 15-16
- religious aspect of, 18-19
- to be understood in context of Arab life, 14-15

Jihād, *jihād – contd.*
  unsatisfactory basis for foreign policy, 19, 91, 92
jiwār, *see* 'neighbourly protection'
jizya, *see* poll-tax
Joseph, 70
judicial
  closing of gate of *ijtihād*, 73
  decisions: basis of, under *qāḍī*, 42; denunciation of those rejecting, 24
  matters:
    absence of independent judicature, 122; administration of in Umayyad period, 41-2; court established by rulers, 76, 95; criminal jurisdiction under police, 76, 95; rise of specialists in, 42, 53; rulers defining sphere of responsibility of judges and courts, 94-5; separate courts for 'protected minorities', 51
jurisprudence
  as the core of higher education, 67
  study of, 70
jurist(s)
  difference between inner reality and juristic expression, 103
  difficulties in producing complete system of law, 66
  hostility between secretaries and, 66-7
  intellectuals, power of in Persia, 112
  rise of, 65-6
  rise of precedent binding, 73
justice
  administration of, in pre-Islamic Arabia, 20
  Muḥammad as arbiter, 21-2, 24
  sureties in legal judgements, 20
  see also arbiter, judicial
al-Juwaynī (Imām al-Ḥaramayn), 106

kāfir, *see* unbeliever
kāhin (soothsayer), 40
Karlowitz, treaty of, 92
al-Kawākibī, 117
Kay Kā'us, 82*
Kennett, A., 135*
Kerbela, 43, 114
Khadduri, M., 140*
khalīfa
  facets of meaning of, 32-3
  occurrence in Qur'ān, 32
  Umayyad caliphs' use of, 33-4
khalīfat rasūl Allāh, 32
kharāj, *see* land-tax
khārij, meaning of, 54
Khārijite(s) (Khawārij)
  as the people of Paradise, 57
  Azraqite: extremism, 55-6; response to, 56
  belief in charismatic community, 55, 56-7, 85
  doctrine of grave sin excluding from community, 55, 57, 58, 62
  emphasis on solidarity of believers, 97
  excellence in poetry and oratory, 57
  independent dynasties, 99
  moderates among, 56
  movement: as expression of social and political discontent, 65; origin of, 54;

Khārijite(s) – *contd.*
political aspect of, 54, 55, 56-7; religious aspect of, 54-5
Murji'ite challenge to, 58
political decisions to be based on Qur'ān, 54-5
revolts against 'Alī, 54
Shī'ite movement compared with, 56
Khaybar
expedition against, 46
Jews accepted into Pax Islamica, 49
Khazraj, 21
Khojas, 114
Khorasanians, 47-8
killing
Azraqite view of, 55-6
blood-wit in cases of accidental, 9
lex talionis as restraint on, 6
kings, divine, of the Yemen, 44, 56
kinship
community superseding claims of, 5
group: and effective working of the *lex talionis*, 6-7; denoted by *qawm*, 11; help for weak groups, 7; modern use of group responsibility, 7; kinsmen of criminal to assist in punishment, 9; responsibility for blood-wit and ransom, 8-9; size of, and effectiveness as operative unit, 11; solidarity of in sharing guilt, 7; *umma* as federation of, 11
knowledge (*'ilm*), 41
Kufa, 43
kufr (unbelief), 62
al-Kulīnī, 143
Kurds, 119
Kuwait, membership of Arab League, 119

lā ḥukm illā li-llāh, 54
Lambton, A. K. S., 143*
Lammens, H., 137*
land
conquered: army not allowed to settle on, 18; continuing in ownership of, 46; used as bases for further razzias, 18
-tax: assignment of, 46; book on, 105; collection of, 18, 50; exaction of, 50
language, as criterion of an Arab, 118
Laoust, H., 107*, 139*, 142*
law
'ancient schools' of, 65-6
association with 'Abbāsid government, 65
bases of legal decisions, 66, 93-4
consensus of community in, 57
customary, 66
different schools of, 66
elaboration of Shī'ite rite, 101
pressure for uniformity in, 65-6, 126
Qur'ānic, 66
rigidity of legal system, 73-4
roots of, 70
study of legal theory, 70
supremacy of the Sharī'a, 67
systematization of, 66, 67, 126
zeal for community producing system of, 59
see also judicial matters, Sharī'a

leadership
'Abbāsid use of imam concept, 45
caliph as war leader, 41
charismatic: 'Abbāsid view of, 39; adaptive change through appearance of, 123-5, 128, 129; belief of autocratic bloc in, 88; in the clan Hāshim, 45; in the family, 35, 110; of the Mahdī, 124-5; Shī'ite concept of, 44, 56, 110
divine kings of the Yemen, 44, 56
importance for succession, 35
in pre-Islamic Arabia, 20, 40
in war, 20, 22-3, 40, 41
Khārijite criticism of, 57
transmission of qualities in families, 35
Umayyad claim of inherited qualities of, 35
Lebanon, membership of the Arab League, 119
Lecomte, G., 139*
legislation
absence of power to legislate, 42, 94, 95
imperial administrative decrees and, 96
Lenin, 121
Levy, R., xi*, 82*
Lewicki, T., 138*
Lewis, B., 141*, 143*
Lewis, I. M., 144*
lexicography, study of, 69
lex talionis
as restraint on killing, 6
kinship group and effective working of, 6-7
modification of, 7, 9
operation of, 6
Libya, membership of the Arab League, 119
Lie, Affair of, 21
linguistic group
concept of in early Islam, 11
umma as applied to, 10
literature
Persian themes in Arabic, 81
stories of Persian kings in Arabic, 81-2
traces of colour-consciousness in mediaeval Arabic, 97
logic, use of, 71, 126-7
luxury
enjoyed by Arabs campaigning, 44, 48
Umayyad indulgence in, 39
Lybyer, A. H., 141*

McCarthy, R. J., 105*
Macdonald, D. B., xi*, 140*, 144*
Madelung, W., 143*
madrasa Niẓāmiyya, 74
maghāẓī (expeditions), 70
see also razzias
Mahdī, Mahdiyya
adaptation through, 124
belief that twelfth imam would return as, 111
conception of, among Shī'ites, 44
of the Sudan: appointment of Khalīfas, 33, 35; movement of, 124
Mahdism
attack on contemporary situation, 124-5
examples of, 124
possible perversion of, 125
use of force, 125
Maḥmūd of Ghazna, 102
mala' (senate), 12

Mālikite school of law, 66
Maltese, 118
Mamlūks
  Burjī, 101
  Baybars' installation of caliph, 108
al-Ma'mūn, caliph
  Inquisition under, 85, 87, 98
  intellectual activities in time of, 88-9
  work of translation organized by, 127
Maqnā, treaty with Jews of, 49
marriage between Muslims and unbelievers, 56
Marx, Marxism, ix, 121-2
Massignon, L., 62, 138*, 139*, 141*
al-Māturīdī, 105
Māturīdite school, 85, 105
Mauritania, 119
mawālī, *mawlā*, *see* clients
al-Māwardī
  aim of, 102
  Gibb's views on, 101-2
  Ordinances of Government, 101-2, 106*
Mecca, Meccan(s)
  as a commercial centre, 3
  Emigrants, *see* Emigrants from Mecca
  merchants: contacts with outside world, 3, 12; effect of Islam on, 3-4; opposition to Islamic ideas, 4
  Muḥammad's struggle against: capture of, 4, 13, 16; community to show solidarity against, 9; first victory over, 15; Meccans' opposition to, 3-4, 11; Muḥammad not 'controller' over, 27; negotiations in, 628, 23; part played by Medinan Muslims in, 4, 13, 15, 22; Qur'ānic exhortation to fight, 15-16, 23-4; razzias against, 13,16
  population in, 610, 3
  prosperity leading to social malaise, 4, 29
  rival caliph in, 37
  senate, 12
  succession question: clans consulted, 39; nomadic tribes' desire for leader from, 31; Umayya, 37
medicine, 71, 126
Medina, Medinan(s)
  benefit from principle of priority of Islam, 47
  clans: alliances with Muḥammad, 4, 13; alliances with nomads, 13; joining into tribes, 21; warfare among, 21
  distinction between Emigrants and Muslims of, 15, 22
  hostilities against Meccans, 4, 13, 15, 22
  Jews: as a natural community, 11; expulsion of clans, 5; groups remaining, 5; treaty with Muḥammad, 49
  nomadic tribes going to live in, 24
  state: desire for local community for religious purposes, 14; part in establishing Islamic, 14; *rasūl* signifying managing affairs of, 27; relevance of Constitution for study of, 5; the pre-Islamic tribes and, 6-9

Medina – *contd.*
succession question: consultation in, 31, 39; meeting on Muḥammad's death, 31-2; unsuitability of a Medinan, 31
see also Constitution of Medina
Messenger of God
caliph of, 32-4
implying practical and political activity, 28
normal appellation of Muḥammad in Qūr'ān, 27
other references, 38, 49, 60, 62, 113-14
Messiah, 44, 124
metaphysics, Greek
rejection of, 127
study of, 71
Mez, A., xi*
Middle East, minority problem in, 51
Miḥna, *see* Inquisition
military
aid: rendering of, 5
élite, Muslims as, 46-9, 52
force: independence through, 99-100; use by Mahdists, 125; war-lords ruling through, 100
leadership: effects of transformation from Arab nomads to, 56-7; in pre-Islamic Arabia, 20; of Muḥammad, 22-3; proportion of proceeds allotted to, 22-3
reform of the Dīwān, 46-7; *see also* army
Miller, W. M., 142*
millet, 50
see also protected minorities
mining, 3
Miqdād-i-Fāḍil, 142
Mirrors for Princes, 81-2
mīthāq, *see* treaty
Mongol sack of Baghdad, 34, 100, 107
morals, morality
army as guardian of nation's, 48-9
conflict between state and individual, 28
muḥtasib's supervision of public, 76, 95
religion and individual, 28
system of, arising from zeal for community, 59
Morocco
independent dynasty in, 99
membership of Arab League, 119
mosque-builders, plot associated with, 25
Muʿāwiya (1)
chosen as person best fitted by experience, 38
civil war between ʿAlī and, 43
claim as avenger of blood, 38
proclaimed as caliph, 37-8
refusal to acknowledge ʿAlī, 37
revolts during reign, 54
statesmanship of, 41
Muʿāwiya II, 39
Muḥammad
ability to handle administrative details, 25
accepted as exemplar and model, 93
adaptive changes effected by, 123-4
appreciation of centrality of need for expansion, 18-19
as arbiter, 21, 26
as charismatic leader, 123-4

Muḥammad – *contd.*
as clan chief, 21
as head of state, 20-30
as Messenger, 21, 24-5, 26
death of, 31
decisions made by, 23-4, 26
declarations, increasing power of, 24-5
desire for local community for religious purposes, 14
disowned by chief Abū-Lahab, 98
Islamic state under, 3-19
military leadership of, 22-3
modifying nomadic ideals and practices, 125-6
obedience to, 23-4
plot against, 25
political achievements of, 3-4
position: in respect of Emigrants, 21, 22; under Constitution, 20-3
power: as head of federation, 25; effect of communal solidarity and, 29; increase through alliances, 24-5, 26; increase through razzias, 24; slow growth of, 4; weakness in first few years in Medina, 21-2
prophethood: charisma of, 123; enhancing suitability as arbiter, 21
situation at death of, 31-5
study of career and expeditions of, 70
views on blood-wit, 9
withdrawal of protection from, 55
Muḥammad Aḥmad, Mahdī of the Sudan, 33, 124
Muhammad ibn-al-Ḥanafiyya, 43, 44, 45
muḥtasib (market inspector), 76, 95
mujtahids, 112, 139
see also *ijtihād*
al-Mukhtār, 43, 45
mulk (kingdom), 39
mu'minūn (believers)
criteria, 60-1
meaning of, 12, 59-60
term confined to Arabs, 61
use of in Qur'ān, 59
al-murābiṭūn, see Almoravids
Murji'ites, 58
Mūsā al-Kāẓim (ʿAlid imam), 112
muṣayṭir, 27
mushrik (polytheist), 11-12, 56
see also *shirk*
Musil, Alois, 7, 8, 135*
Muslim (name of Traditionist), 93
Muslim(s)
as military élite, 46-9
membership of state confined to, 14
proper application of word, 60
muslimūn
islām as verbal noun of, 60
meaning of, 59
use of in Qur'ān, 59
Mustafa Kemal Atatürk, 109
al-Mustaʿli (Fāṭimid), 114
Mustaʿlians, 114
al-Mustanṣir (Fāṭimid), 114
al-Mustaẓhir, caliph, 106
al-Muʿtaṣim, caliph, 48
al-Mutawakkil (I), caliph, 85, 87
al-Mutawakkil III, caliph, 108
Muʿtazilites
advocacy of the createdness of the Qur'ān, 88
similarity of Zaydite views to, 115

Mu'tazilites – *contd.*
  use of Greek argument, 71, 127
muwaḥḥid (monotheist), 56
al-muwaḥḥidūn, *see* Almohads

an-Naḍīr, 5
Najjar, F. M., 142*
Najm-ad-Dīn an-Nasafī, 105
Nallino, C., 137*
an-nāsikh wa-l-mansūkh (abrogation), 94
Naṣīr-ad-Dīn Ṭūsī, 106
naṣṣ, *see* designation
Nasser, Gamal Abd-an-, 118
nationalism
  Arab, 117, 118-19
  Egyptian, 118
  hypothetical Ottoman, 117
  Imāmism as basis for Persian, 112, 117
  independence and, 117, 119
  in Islam, 116-20
  Pakistani, 119-20
  secular Islamic, 120
  Turkish, 117
  usefulness in struggle against colonialism, 116-17
an-Nawbakhtī, 143
naẓar fī-l-maẓālim, 76
'neighbourly protection' (*jiwār*)
  as strengthening the group, 8
  community to show solidarity in granting, 5, 8, 9
  grant of, by single person, 8
Neoplatonism, 71, 81, 106, 127
neutrality, impossible in Islam, 16
New Testament, 6, 27, 49
  see also Bible
Nicholson, R. A., 140*
Nietzsche, 129
Nigeria, Northern, 124
Niẓām-al-Mulk (vizier), 74, 82*, 106
Niẓāmiyya (college), 74
Nizār, 114
Nizārian Ismā'īlites, 114
nobility
  conflict of interests within old, 47
  creation of military, 46-9
  pre-Islamic concept of, 57
  Sharī'a conferring on community, 91
  waqf system creating, 79-80
nobility of action, 90
Nöldeke, Th., 136*
nomadic tribes
  alliances with Medinan clans, 13
  alliances with Muḥammad, 4, 24
  belief that safety lies in following the *sunna*, 123
  communal solidarity among, 29
  effects of transformation to military élite, 56-7
  going to live in Medina, 24
  mores: influence of in Constitution, 5-6; tension between commercial interests and, 4
  political concepts unsuited to empire, 29
  resistance to change, 123; *see also* Arabs
non-aggression pacts, 13
North
  Africa: disappearance of Christianity from, 52; Muslim expansion through, 18
  Arabia, reverence for tribe in, 56
an-Nu'mān, Qāḍī, 106*

oaths
  taken before arbiters, 20
  taken by clients, 8
obedience
  as carrying out Qur'ānic prescriptions, 23-4
  as condition in declarations, 24
  in moral matters, 23
  to imam, 44
  to caliphate, Umayyad claims concerning, 38
Old Testament, 49, 123
  see also Bible
Oman, 56
oratory, 57
Ottoman
  adoption of European institutions, 116
  caliphate: abolition of, 35, 109; adoption of, 34-5, 108; Muslim recognition of, 108-9; resurrection of, 109
  Christians under empire, 52
  conquest of Egypt, 108
  nationalism, 117
  proclamation of *jihād*, 19
  proposal that 'protected minorities' share nationality, 48
  slave-households, 29, 101
  use of *qānūn*, 96

pagan Arabs
  choice between Islam and the sword, 16, 50-1
  option of becoming a protected community, 16-17
Pakistan
  constitutive element of nationhood, 119-20
  Islamic constitution of, 121
  position in relation to sphere of Islam, 92
Palestine, 27
Paret, R., 136*
patience, 97
patron, 7-8
Patton, W. M., 140*
Pax Islamica, extension of, 18
peace, community's relations with unbelievers in, 5, 9
Pellat, Ch., 82*, 140*
Persia, Persian(s)
  administration: adoption of form of, 29; breakdown of 13-14; increased influence of, 79-80; provincial, 12; Umayyad interest in, 79
  asceticism, 83
  client status, resentment at, 78
  cultural: borrowing from, 71; heritage, 80; superiority, belief in, 83; traditions, readiness to accept, 80-1
  element in autocratic bloc, 83
  Imāmism: as official religion of, 111-12, 117; basis for development of nationalism in, 112, 117; effect of isolating Persia, 112
  imperial tradition, 78-82
  independent dynasties in, 99
  Isaac as ancestor of, 89
  Ismā'īlite movement in, 113-14
  literature: translated into Arabic, 81; works on art of ruling, 81-2
  Meccan: contacts with provincial administration, 12, 71; trade with, 3
  power of *mujtahids*, 112
  nationalism, 112, 117

Persia, Persian(s) – *contd.*
prerogative of investigating complaints derived from, 95
recruited to army, 47-8
religious homogeneity of, 112
Shāh, religio-political position of, 112
Shīʿite associations with, 44, 83, 111-12, 117
statecraft, 81-2
support of ʿAbbāsids, 78
tradition in political theory, 105
vizierate, 80
Petersen, E. L., 137*
Philosophers, 127, 128
philosophy
Greek: acceptance of, 81; adaptation of, 16-17; translation of, 71; use of, 88
Islamic, 71, 127
Neoplatonism, 71, 106, 127
Pledge of Good Pleasure
accounts of, 23, 136
interpretation of, 25-6
Plato, 81, 104
see also Neoplatonism
plot against Muḥammad, 25
poetry
collection of old Arabic, 69
cultivation of, 70
effect of the Shuʿūbite movement, 83
excellence of Khārijite, 57
pre-Islamic, extolling noble deeds, 90
satire in Arabic, 83
Poitiers, battle of, 17
police courts, 95
political
concepts: deficiency of Arabism in, 79; influence of pre-Islamic on Constitution, 6; new, derived from regions conquered, 29-30; nomadic, unsuited to empire, 29; of the pre-Islamic Arabs, 6-9; presupposing expansion, 91-2; region of origin of religion influencing, 29; structure of Islamic state based on pre-Islamic, 14; roots of, operative in Islam today, ix; traditional, 92
discontent expressed in Khārijite movement, 65
forces, ix
heritage, likelihood of Islam remaining faithful to, 129
ideas: Islam and occidental, 116-23; operative in historical process, x; of pre-Islamic Arabia based on tribal system, 12, 68
life, controlled by age-old patterns, 123
organization, relevance of Islam to, 28
power of Muḥammad, *see* Muḥammad
quietism of nascent Christianity, 27
relevance of religion, 26-30
relevance of religious discussion, 65
structure conceived in Qur'ānic terms, 68
struggle, the form of the, 78-89
theorists: preliminary list of, 104-7; war-lords and, 99-109
theory: absence of, 5, 81;

political theory – *contd.*
as of secondary importance to practice, x, 101-2; expressed in the form of history, 36-7; Gibb's view of Sunnite, 103-4; need for study of the history of, 104; place of spheres in, 91-2; relation to historical reality, 104; 'standard' account of, 101-2; Sunnite, 102-3; writings on, x
thought: influence of philosophers on, 104; refusal to be bound by formulae, 103-4
unit, *qawm* denoting, 11
unity: dream of pan-Islamism, 120; means of advancing, 30; new and greater, through adaptation, 125
writing, Muslim, of the 19th and 20th c., 116
politics
contribution of Khārijite ideas to, 56-7
early Islam as irrelevant to, 3
historical discussions arising from contemporary, 86
involvement of religion in man's, 26-7
Islam in contemporary, 116-29
personal element in Arab, 120-1
poll-tax (*jizya*)
assignment of, 46
collection of, 52
exaction of, 50
paid by protected groups, 42
polygamy, 35
polytheists
definition of, 56
probable alliances with Muḥammad, 11-12
power struggle
historical ideas, 86-7
intellectual form of, 85-9
theological ideas, 87-8
under the first ʿAbbāsids, 82-5
practice
more important than theory, x, 101-2
relation of Sunnite to political theory, 102-3
pregnancies, 95
pre-Islamic Arabia
administration of justice in, 20
amount allotted to war leaders, 22-3
belief in decree of Fate, 38
caliphate conceived on triba ideas of, 40-1
concept of nobility, 57, 90
effective protection as an honour, 51
ideas unsuited to empire, 39-40
maintenance of security in, 6-7
mores and mentality, influencing Constitution, 5-6
Muḥammad's: position in community based on ideas of, 20; state conceived as tribe of, 14
political concepts of, 6
relevance of concepts to body politic, 12-13
succession in, 35
tribe: and the Medinan state, 6-9; expulsion of deviants from, 98

pre-Islamic Arabia – *contd.*
  tribal government in, 20, 40-1
  Umayyad: following of custom of, 65, 66; rule based on ideas of, 39-40
  view of history, 68
  war leadership in, 20
  world-view, 68
primogeniture, absence of law of, 35, 101
propagandists, 72
prophethood
  caliph's lack of, 42
  charisma of, 123
  enhancing Muḥammad's suitability as arbiter, 21
  nature of Muḥammad's, 27-8
  prophet: as a European appellation, 27; contrasted with Messenger of God, 28; 'protected minority' only offered to followers of, 50-1
'protected minorities' (*ahl adh-dhimma*: *dhimmīs*)
  action of, of no significance to Islam, 71
  advantages of, 51
  as an option to those defeated by Muḥammad, 16
  as bases for further razzias, 18
  assumption of religious homogeneity, 50
  conquered accepting status of, 18
  conversion to Islam, 51-2
  definition of, 8
  disadvantages of, 51-2
  dwindling numbers of, 51
  effect of Islamic world-view on, 72
  effective protection and honour, 51
  exaction of land-tax and poll-tax, 18, 50, 52
  excluded from military service, 48-9
  method of conferring, 8
  origin of, 50
  Ottoman: proposal to share nationality, 48; term 'millet' used for, 50
  payment of tribute, 49, 50
  privilege only accorded to those following a prophet, 50-1
  protection from external enemies, 49, 50
  regulations concerning, 49-52
  retention of internal government, 49, 50, 52
  separate courts for, 51
  voluntary and forced submission, 50
protection
  alternative, 55
  among Rwala, 8
  Arab practice extended to minorities, 49-50
  and honour, 8, 51
  as an obligation, 8
  concept of among true Bedouin, 8
  conception of *jihād* introducing expanding sphere of, 17-18
  conception of, leading to expansion of the Islamic state, 17
  effect of growing strength of community on, 16
  in matters other than killing, 9
  maintenance of, as a matter of honour, 49-50
  of community, importance of, 55

protection – *contd.*
  of God and his prophet, 16
  operation of the razzia and, 16
  solidarity of group and individual, 7
  system of security influencing concept of, 7-8
  through Muḥammad's declaration, 24
  under the sphere of truce, 91-2
  withdrawal from, 55
Protestant Christianity, as a political force of the future, ix
provincial administration
  administration through the army, 52
  changes in details of, 53
  generals responsible for Muslims only, 52
  of Byzantium and Persia, 12
punishment
  administered by Muḥammad, 25
  kinsmen of criminal to assist in securing, 9
  need to carry out effectively, 6
  of crime: Murji'ite justification of, 58; theologians' view of, 58-9
  terminated by Qur'ānic revelation, 25
Punjab, 40

qaḍā, 24
qāḍī (judge)
  appointed from 'ancient schools of law', 65
  basis of decisions under, 42
  development of office of, 41
  form of appeal from, 76
  posts in imperial gift, 73
  provincial, 53
  rise of specialists among, 42, 53
  rulers' power to appoint, 94
  rulers' power to define competence of, 95
Qāḍī an-Nuʿmān, 106
Qādisiyya, battle of, 47
qā'id, *see* war-leader
qānūn, 96
Qarāmiṭa, 112-13
Qaynuqāʿ, expulsion of clan from Medina, 5
qawm (tribe)
  and *umma*, 11
  as a natural community, 11
  consisting mainly of unbelievers, 12
  meaning of, 11
  Muḥammad's message addressed to, 27
  use of in Qur'ān, 11, 12
Qur'ān
  amplifying provisions of Constitution, 9
  createdness of, 73, 87, 88
  decisions implementing commands of, 26
  disciplines arising from need to understand, 69
  elaboration of ideas into world-view, 69
  exhortation to join razzia, 22
  influence of ideas on Arabs, 68
  legal rules in, 66
  political potential of ideas realized at Medina, 4
  prescriptions: on portion of war proceeds, 22-3; on uses of war proceeds, 22
  religious ideas directed at malaise in Mecca, 4

Qur'ān – *contd.*
revelations and Muḥammad's administration, 25
revelation held as complete, 42
rise of exegesis, 69
Quraysh, tribe of, 31
Qurayẓa, clan of
expulsion from Medina, 5
punishment of, 22

racial discrimination, 97
Rāfiḍites, 110
ransom
responsibility of each clan, 5, 30
responsibility of kinship groups for, 8-9
rāshidūn (rightly-guided, *sc.*, caliphs)
accession of, 35-6, 38
as the golden age of the caliphate, 36
history of, rewritten to incorporate ideals, 36-7
rasūl Allāh, 27, 32
razzias (*maghāzī*)
aim of, 15
alliances limiting scope of, 17
Arab conquest as an extension of, 17
Arab system of protection and operation of, 16
as a feature of Arab life, 16
booty as a primary feature of, 17, 18
character of, 15
conception of *jihād* and, 17-18
decisions in respect of particular, 26
expanding sphere of protection, 17-18
extension of, 17
increase in Muḥammad's power through, 24
jihād as development of, 18
leadership of, 22-3
Medinan period as series of, 15
Muḥammad's against Meccan caravans, 13, 70
need to extend field of, 17, 18-19
not to be directed against community or its allies, 16
of Iraqi tribes on Southern Iraq, 14
'protected minorities' used as bases for further, 18
Qur'ānic exhortation to join, 15, 22
religious and materialistic aspects of, 18
rules of, 15
undertaken by Emigrants from Mecca, 15-16, 22
word given religious significance, 16
refutation, 72
Reischauer, R. D., 138*
religion
absence of political relevance in early Islam, 3
activities influenced by, 28
accidental political effects of, 30
adopting political concepts from regions conquered, 29
as a factor motivating agreement, 14
as a potential basis for political interference, 3-4
as concerned only with personal piety, ix
aspect of the *jihād*, 18-19

religion – *contd.*
assumption that natural communities share same rites, 11
communal concept of, 28-9
concept of state where religion could be practised, 14
confining membership to Muslims, 14
contrast between *dīn* and, 29
dominance of, after Muḥammad's death, 64-5
duties of caliphs, 42
element in Mahdism, 124-5
favouring political concepts of region of origin, 29
generating motives for activity, 28
ideas influencing life of society, x
ideology with functions of, ix
individual morality and, 28
involvement of, in man's social and political life, 26-7
link with politics through war, ix
local community for, 14
occidental concept of, ix
political relevance of, 26-30
razzias and, 16, 18
resistance to change, 123
warnings that political activity would be necessary, 27
religious institution
ʿAbbāsid support of, 73, 74
alliance with Seljūqs, 74
and the rulers, 73-7
'ancient schools of law', 65-6
as part of the establishment, 122
as recognized exponents of the Sharīʿa, 67
Buwayhid influence on, 74
challenge of the dervish orders, 76-7
creation of established order of security, 76
decrease in influence of, 76
establishment of, 67
establishment of colleges, 74-5
extent of achievement of, 75
formation of, 64-67
ʿ*ilm* of scholars replacing wisdom of arbiters, 41
incomplete recognition by rulers, 75
influence of European impact on, 75
maintenance of degree of independence, 122
political working of the church performed through, 64
producing Islamic world-view, 67-8
replacement by new body of intellectuals, 77
role of discussion in rise of, 64-5
role of ulema in, 67
rivalry with secretaries, 74
subservience to rulers, 73
support of bulk of population for, 84
supremacy of, in intellectualism, 71
triumph of, 74-5
ulema yielding to rulers, 75
weakness of, 73-4
rents, 18, 42
revenge
as a sacred duty of the group, 6

revenge – *contd.*
  duty of, required for public security, 6
  duty to avenge ʿUthmān, 54
  exacting of, 6-7
  Muʿāwiya as avenger of ʿUthmān, 38
  need to carry out effectively, 6
  sharing of guilt and exaction of, 7
  Umayyad use of, 39, 54
reversion, 44
Richter, G., 139*
ridda (apostasy), 62
rights of man, 96, 121
rightly-guided, see *rāshidūn*
Robson, J., 140*
Roman(s), 27, 70, 72, 81, 89
Rosenthal, E. I. J., 139*
Rosenthal, F., 141*, 143*
Rubinacci, R., 138*
rulers
  absence of legislative power, 42, 94, 95
  avoidance of rebellion against *de facto*, 58, 97
  prerogative of investigating complaints, 95
  powers to define responsibility of courts, 94-5
  use of decrees, 95, 96
  use of force to achieve conformity, 98
  view that some government is better than no government, 97
Rwala tribe, 7, 8

Sabʿiyya, *see* Ismāʿīlites
ṣabr (patience), 97
Saʿd ibn-ʿUbāda, 31, 32
Ṣafavid dynasty, 112
Ṣaffārid dynasty, 99
ṣalāt (worship), 60
salvation, 91
Sāmānid dynasty, 99
Samarqand, 40
Sasanian, Sasanid (pre-Islamic Persian dynasty)
  approval of form of government, 78
  empire, administration in, 66
  origin of 'protected minorities', 50
  secretaries employed by, 82
Saʿudi Arabia, membership of Arab League, 119
sayyid (chief)
  consultation with notables, 41
  disputes referred to, 40-1
  limitations on powers of, 20, 40-1
  Muḥammad as *sayyid* of the Emigrants, 21
  powers of, in pre-Islamic Arabia, 40
Schacht, J., 137*
science
  assimilation of European scientific thought, 128-9
  study of, 71, 126
secretaries
  as a hereditary class, 80, 82
  as an element in the autocratic bloc, 67
  defined, 66
  effect of createdness of Qur'ān on role of, 88
  employment of Iraqi, 79
  hostility to jurists, 66-7, 74
  Ibn-al-Muqaffaʿ as representative of, 81, 82
  opportunity to increase power, 82
  posts in central administration, 82

secretaries—*contd.*
reasons for desire for autocracy, 67
requirement to be Muslims, 82
rivalry with ulema, 88
training of, 80
triumph of ulema over, 74-5
security
attained through obedience to charismatic leader, 110
concept of protection influenced by system of, 7-8
duty to help and revenge required for public, 6
guarantee of, under sphere of truce, 91-2
lack of, expressed in Shī'ite and Khārijite movements, 56
lex talionis as primitive method of maintaining, 6
purpose of government to maintain, 91, 96
self-esteem, 18
Seljūqs
appointment of tutor-guardians, 101
capture of Baghdad, 74, 100
Sunnite sympathies of, 101
senate of Mecca, 12
sending to Coventry, 25
Serjeant, R. B., 135*
sermon, Friday
delivered by caliphs, 42
political potential of, 30
Seveners, *see* Ismā'īlite(s)
ash-Shāfi'ī, 66, 93-4
Shāfi'ite school of law, 66, 107
shahāda, *see* confession of faith
Sharī'a (Islamic law)
'Abbāsids desire for uniformity in, 65-6, 126
all Muslims subject to, 122
approved practices to be justified by reference to Muḥammad, 126
as divinely-revealed law, 67, 94
as ideal law, 94
as proceeding from the will of the people, 121
caliphate a symbol of supremacy of, 102
caliph's relations with ministers outwith, 75
charismatic nature of community and, 102-3
circles of pious men discussing, 126
conferring solidarity on community, 91
constitution in accordance with central principles of, 121
constitutionalist bloc's belief in government through, 88
controlling structure of society, 75
creation of, as an adaptation of the intellectuals, 125-6
diminished sphere of influence, 95
dominance of, securing benefits of independent judicature, 122
emphasis on equality, 78-9
existence of as divinely-given *sunna* of social life, 123
inadequacy of, in modern times, 122
limitations of, 75
maintenance of supremacy of, 103
matters included in, 94

Sharīʿa – *contd.*
modification of, 95, 125-6
possibility of salvation through, 91
Qur'ān and Sunna determining, 84, 91, 94
rigidity of, 75
rival jurisdictions, 76
totalitarianism prevented by, 122
ulema as only authorized interpreters of, 94
urgency about adaptation of, 122
weakness in interests of ordinary people, 121
work of systematization, 126
shaykh, 20, see also *sayyid*
ash-Shaykh aṣ-Ṣadūq al-Qummī, 106
Sherwani, H. K., 141*
Shīʿa, meaning of, 43
Shīʿism, Shīʿites
ʿAlid group and, 110, 111
association with ʿAlī, 43
association with al-Fārābī, 105
attempts of rulers to gain approval of, 83
belief in charismatic leader, 110, 124
claim for ʿAlī to succeed, 31, 83, 86
claim of special powers for clan of Hāshim, 43
effect of Imāmite in Persia, 112
elaboration of legal rite, 101
element in autocratic bloc, 83, 110
erroneous views concerning, 86-7
Fāṭimid form of Ismāʿīlite, 105-6
first appearance of ideas, 42-5
formation of ulema, 74
Imāmite: creed, 106; designation by predecessor, 86; official religion of Persia, 111-12
Islam, development of, 110-15
moderate and the Imāmite party, 110-12
Muʿtazilite sympathy with, 88
origin of, 42-3, 83
reasons for rise of, 44
rewriting of history, 43
revolts against the Umayyads, 43
Revolutionary or Sevener, 112-14
search for charismatic leader, 56, 115; support of ʿAbbāsids, 78, 83
sympathies of Buwayhids, 101
view of imam's inherited powers, 43-4
Yemenite origin of, 44
Zaydite, 114-15
shirk (idolatry), 62
see also polytheists
shūrā (council), 35-6
shurṭā (police), 76
Shuʿūbite movement, 83
sin
grave, excluding from community, 55, 57; making an infidel, 62; political effects of, 55-6; tendency to reduce number of, 58
not excluding from membership, 58
Murji'ite view of, 58
sīra (biography), 70
slaves
becoming clients on emancipation, 7-8

slaves – *contd.*
freeing of, for accidental killing, 9
household, 29, 101
man as slave of God, 97
selling of girls as concubines to unbelievers, 58
Smith, W. C., 140*, 144*
social
discontent: adaptation of society through reform of, 124-5; expressed in Khārijite movement, 65
effect of Qur'ānic ideas, 4
malaise in Mecca, 4
organization, relevance of Islam to, 28
relevance of religious discussion to, 65
unit, *qawm* as, 11
socialism
African, 122
question of Islamic, 122-3
society
controlled by Sharī'a, 75
loyalty to Islam, 120
practices of, intellectuals' attempts to bring nearer western, 128
Sokoto, sultanate of, 124
solidarity
communal, *see* communal solidarity
effective working of *lex talionis* and, 6-7
fostering of, as essence of Islam, 30
independent of religious system, 98
in granting neighbourly protection, 5, 9
Islamic attempts to express, politically inadequate, 120
making deviants conform, 97-8
of: believers, 18-19, 97; kinship group, 7; tribe, 12, 97; Umayyad family, 39; *umma*, 29-30, 123
reality of Islamic, 120
sense of, below conceptual level, 98
soothsayer, 40
Sourdel, D., 139*
South Arabia, 33, 44, 56
see also Yemen
Spain
Almohad rule in, 124
independent dynasty in, 99
Muslim expansion through, 18
Umayyad use of titles in, 34
'spheres'
definition of, 91
discussion of three, 91-2
Stalin, 121
state
birth of the Islamic, 4
concept of place where religion could be practised, 14
concept of protection leading to expansion of, 17
Islamic under Muḥammad, 3-19
Muḥammad as head of, 20-30
Muḥammad as autocrat in external affairs, 26
nature of, defined in Constitution, 5
structure of, based on pre-Islamic ideas, 14, 20
the pre-Islamic tribe and the Medinan, 6-9
see also body politic
Steinschneider, M., 144*
Stern, S. H., 135*

stipends
  end of system, 48, 78
  under the Dīwān, 46-7
Strothmann, R., 143*
succession
  absence of law of primogeniture, 35, 101
  acclamation, 35, 36, 37, 38, 39, 86
  appointment of Abū-Bakr, 32
  appointment of council, 35-6
  Arab practice in, 31
  Arbitration on, 37-8
  'best among the Muslims', 3, 39
  consultation, 35, 37, 38, 39
  designation, 35, 37, 39, 86
  historical arguments in the power struggle, 86
  in pre-Islamic Arabia, 35
  khalīfa signifying, 32, 33
  new form practised by Umayyads, 37
  polygamy complicating problem of, 35
  problem of assessing ages, 35
  problem of, with war-lords, 101
  qualities of leadership important for, 35
  standard account of accession of the *rāshidūn*, 35-6
  Sunnite view of, 42
  to the caliphate, 35-40
  tutor-guardian experiment, 101
  Umayyad arguments substantiating claims, 38
Sudan
  Communist party unlawful in, ix, 122
  Islamic constitution of, 121
  Mahdī of the, 33, 35, 124
  membership of the Arab League, 119
ṣulḥan, 50
sulṭān (authority, war-lord), 100
Sumer(ian), 10, 80
Sunna, 84, 91, 94, 123-4
Sunnism, Sunnite
  'Abbāsid commitment to, 111
  as an adaptation of the intellectuals, 125-6
  belief in charismatic community, 85
  element in constitutionalist bloc, 84
  dominance of form of Islam, 67
  establishment of, 82, 85, 90
  Gibb's view of political thought, 103-4
  inauguration of intellectual schools of theology, 85
  influence of the Seljūqs, 74, 101
  life of the empire to be based on Sharī'a, 84-5
  meaning of, 84
  political theory of, 102-3
  regard for *rāshidūn*, 36
  roots of political thinking, 115
  successful appearance of charismatic leaders in regions of, 124
  values and ideals expressed in Traditions, 93
suras quoted
  2.30/28, 33
  2.143/37, 10
  4.59/62, 34
  4.92/4, 9, 11
  4.93/5, 9
  5.35/9, 15

suras quoted – *contd.*
7.38/6, 10
8.72/3, 15
9.118/9, 25
12, 70
16.110/1, 15
33.36, 24
37.102/0-113, 89
38.26/5, 33
42.41/39, 9
48.18, 23
52.32, 11
69.7, 11
88.22, 27
Syria
attempt to develop local nationalism, 118
expeditions against, 17, 18-19
Greek intellectual heritage of, 126
intellectual contacts through conquest, 68
Ismā'īlite movement in, 113-14
membership of the Arab League, 119
translations from, 126-7
Syriac language, 127

aṭ-Ṭabarī, 81
Tabūk, 24, 49
tafsīr (exegesis), 69
at-Taftazānī, 142*
taḥāluf, *see* alliance
Ṭāhir, 99
Ṭāhirid dynasty, 99
taḥrīf (corruption, *sc.* of scriptures), 69, 72
takfīr (declaration of unbelief), 62
taqlīd (following of precedents), 94
taxes, 18
teaching
of administrators, 74-5
use of formal, 65
theology
aspect of the power struggle, 87-9
expounding new views to start *jihād*, 19
philosophical concepts in Sunnite, 71
use of Greek argument, 127
Thomas, Bertram, 14, 136*
Thompson, J. H., 138*
tithe
as a condition of declaration, 24
collection by Muḥammad, 25
payment of: as a criterion of a believer, 60; on accepting Islam, 13; under alliance, 13
toleration, 51
Torah, 49
totalitarianism, 121-2
Tours, battle of, 17
Toynbee, Arnold, 26
Traditions (*ḥadīth*)
all legal decisions to be based on, 93-4
authentication of, 66, 70, 93
collecting for legal purposes, 94
collections of, 93
decisions based on, 66
formation of the canon of sound, 85, 93, 126
function of Muslim critique of, 93-4
incorporation of old wisdom in, 72
intellectual effort behind, 126
meaning of, 66, 93
place of, in world-view, 70
potentiality of adaptation, 94

Traditions – *contd.*
refutation, 72
repetition of spurious, 72
study of, 70
Sunnite view of, 84
transmitters of, 66, 70, 93
Trans-Jordan, membership of Arab League, 119
treasury
caliph in charge of, 42
state, 12
treaty
between Muḥammad and the tribes, 13
between Muslims and non-Muslims, 11-12
use of *jamāʿa* in, 12
with Jews and Christians, 49
tribe
as bearer of values, 90
as the body politic, 12
chief of, see *sayyid*
concept of, at centre of early political thinking, 12
councils of, 40
democratic element in, 120
desire to maintain honour of, 90
expulsion of deviants from, 97
functions of, performed by Islamic community, 91
government of, in pre-Islamic Arabia, 90
hostility of, to all others, 16-17
ideal of nobility, 90
negotiations with other tribes, 20
pre-Islamic conception of, 90
regard for, among Khārijites, 56
solidarity of, and political thinking, 12
solidarity of, continued in sense of brotherhood, 97
system of, political ideas based on, 68
the pre-Islamic and the Medinan state, 6-9
use of *qawm* to denote, 11
Tritton, A. S., 138*
Tunisia
as a hereditary governorship, 99
Fāṭimid state in, 34, 112-13
Morocco and, membership of Arab League, 119
Turkey, Turkish
mercenaries, 48, 100
nationalism, 117
need for support, against troops, 89
slave-households, 29, 101
aṭ-Ṭurṭūshī, 140*
tutor-guardians, 101
Twelvers, *see* Imāmite party
Tyan, E., 137*

ulema (*ʿulamāʾ*)
ʿAbbāsid compromise with, 102
achievement of adaptation in social matters, 128
adaptation through, 125-6
as accredited exponents of the Sharīʿa, 85, 88, 94
belief in government in accordance with Sharīʿa, 88
conditions of work, 76
control of higher education, 67, 74
control of social fabric, 102
disinterestedness in other aspects of government, 96, 102

ulema – *contd.*
effect of: createdness of the Qur'ān on role of, 88; Inquisition, 73; *waqf* system, 73
element in the constitutionalist bloc, 84
interest in maintaining charismatic nature of community, 102
looking after interests of ordinary people, 121
loss of moral leadership, 77
perversion of scholarship, 76
placation of, 102
rivalry with secretaries, 88
signs of closer contact with modern intellectuals, 128-9
support of masses for, 84, 93
triumph of, 74-5
values and ideals of, expressed in Traditions, 93
weakness of position, 73
yielding to rulers, 75
ʿUmar (1) (ʿUmar ibn-al-Khaṭṭāb)
autocratic bloc view of, 86
credited with concealing death of Muḥammad, 31
death of, 35
designated caliph by Abū-Bakr, 35
Dīwān of, 46-7
intervention in question of Muḥammad's successor, 31
titles of, 34
Umayya (family, clan), Umayyad dynasty
achievements of, 41
clan including good business men, 36
difficulties in pursuing steady policy, 41
duty to revenge in claim, 39, 54
dynasty in Spain, 99
failure of administration, 39-40
family solidarity of, 39
following of pre-Islamic custom, 65
form of succession practised by, 37-8
interest in Persian administration, 79
manipulation of Arab institutions, 39
methods by which caliphate was retained, 39-40
Murj'iite view of as *de facto* rulers, 58
ousting of, by ʿAbbāsids, 45
personal attributes of, 39-40
pious opposition to, 65
representing old nobility, 47
Shīʿite revolts against, 43
struggle with Ibn-az-Zubayr, 55, 56
use of title of caliph, 33-4
ʿUthmān's membership of family, 36
umma
as a federation of kinship groups, 11
as a natural community, 11
as applied to group not pre-Islamic, 14
date of use in Qur'ān, 10, 12
denoting ethnic, linguistic or confessional group, 10
derivation of, 9-10
history of use of, 10
meaning of, 9-10
Muḥammad not chief of, 20-1
Muḥammad's message addressed to, 27

umma – contd.
qawm and, 11, 12
real solidarity of, 123
reasons for change in meaning, 11
religious connotations of, 10
solidarity of, as chief contribution to political sphere, 29-30
use of, in Constitution, 5, 9, 10, 14
unbelievers (*mushrikūn*)
as opposed to *mu'minūn*, 62
community to show complete solidarity against, 5, 9
declaration of unbelief, 62
definition of, 56
Khārijite discussion on, 56
person outside Islamic community, 62
United Nations, 92
Usuman dan-Fodio, 124
ʿUthmān (caliph)
death of, 36, 37
duty of revenge of, 54
election as caliph, 35-6
Khārijite support of murder of, 54-5
Shīʿite view of, 86
tensions in reign of, 36
ʿUthmānites, 87

values
community as bearer of, 90-8
Traditions as expressions of, 93
tribe as bearer of, 90
van Arendonk, C., 144*
Vatikiotis, P. J., 143*
Veccia Vaglieri, L., 137*
vengeance, *see* revenge
Veselý, R., 138*
vizier, 80
Von Grunebaum, G.E., xi*, 138*
Von Kremer, A., xi*

waqf (religious trust)
administration of, 73
creating hereditary upper class, 79-80
war
as prescribed in Qur'ān, 23-4
civil, following the murder of ʿUthmān, 64
community to show solidarity in, against unbelievers, 5, 9
increase in Muḥammad's power through, 24
linking politics and religion, ix
Qur'ānic prescription on:
payment of fifth to Muḥammad, 22; uses of proceeds of, 22-3
war-leaders
caliphs as, 41
functions of, 20
Muḥammad as, 22-3
tribal, 20, 40
war-lords
and the political theorists, 99-104
as potential guarantors of the Sharīʿa, 103
emergence of the, 99-101
principle of succession, 101
rule in Baghdad, 100
subordination to caliph, 100, 101
theory underlying position of, 100-1
use of term, 100
Wars of the Apostasy, 64
warner, warnings, 27

Watt, W. M., 135*, 136*, 137*, 138*, 139*, 140*, 143*
wazīr, 80
Wellhausen, J., 65, 138*
Wensinck, A. J., 105*
Wickens, G. M., 142*
wine-drinking
  Qur'ānic injunction against, 23
  Umayyad indulgence in, 39
women
  blood-wit for, 7
  changes in position of, 128
world-view, weltanschauung
  borrowing from cultures, 69, 70, 71, 80-1
  disciplines studied, 69-70
  effect of Arab self-confidence on, 71-2
  effect of theory of corruption, 69
  factors leading to dominance of, 68-70
  formation of the, 67-73
  incorporation of Greek culture, 71
  incorporation of old wisdom in, 72
  Islamic, success of, 72-3
  need for elaborated, 69
  of pre-Islamic Arabs, 68
  place of Traditions in, 70
  rejection of other views, 72
  religious institution producing, 67-8, 71
worship
  practice of, as criterion of believer, 60
  purpose of government to afford security for, 96
wufūd (deputations), 39

Xerxes, 80

Yarmuk, battle of, 47
Yathrib (Medina), 130, 133
Yemen
  membership of Arab League, 119
  Shī'ite ideas originating in, 44
  Zaydite state in, 115

zakāt, *see* tithe
zandaqa, 62, 83
Zayd (ibn-'Alī), 114
Zayd ibn-Ḥāritha, 31
Zaydism, 114-15
Zoroastrians, 51, 83